HEARTBEAT GEOGRAPHY

HEARTBEAT GEOGRAPHY

SELECTED & UNCOLLECTED POEMS

JOHN BRANDI

WHITE PINE PRESS · FREDONIA, NEW YORK

Acknowledgements: I am grateful to the editors of the following magazines and presses who
have published some of these poems, or earlier versions:

Am Here Books, *Amaranth Review, American Poets Say Goodbye to the Twentieth Century*
(anthology), *Amerus, And, Atticus, Atomic Ghost* (anthology), *Berkeley Works, Bezoar,
Blaketimes, Blue Mesa Review, Caliban, Chelsea,* Cherry Valley Editions, Christopher Books,
Contact II, Coyote's Journal (anthology), *Crossing the River* (anthology), *Crosswinds,* Distant
Longing Publications, *Don Quichotte* (Lausanne), Duende Press, *Edge, El Palacio, El Salto
Leap, Fervent Valley,* The Figures Press, *Fish Drum,* Floating Island Publications,
Gegenschein, The Great Blafigria Is, Great Raven Books, *Green Fuse, Handbook,* Holy Cow!
Press, *I Sing the Song of Myself* (anthology), *The Indian Rio Grande* (anthology), *Io, Iron*
(Great Britain), *Isthmus, Kuksu,* L.A. Free Press, Light and Dust Books, *Longhouse,
Mendocino Grapevine,* The Nail Press, *Neon, New Life News, New Mexico Magazine, New
Mexico Humanities Review, New Mexico Poetry Renaissance* (anthology), *Nexus, The Northern
Review, Nuke Rebuke* (anthology), *Pax, Peace or Perish* (anthology), *Poetry Flash, Poets On,
Poetry: San Francisco Quarterly, Portland State Review, Puerto del Sol, Resiembra, River Styx,
Rocky Mountain Review, Saludos!* (anthology), *Seen from Space, Semiotext(e) USA, Scree,
Southwest: A Contemporary Anthology, Sparks of Fire: Blake in a New Age* (anthology), *The
Spirit That Moves Us, Stiletto, Stooge, Talus, The Taos Review, The Third Wind, Third Rail,
Tin Wreath,* Tooth of Time Books, Toothpaste Press, *Trapani Nuova* (Italy), Tree Books,
Tribal Press, *Tyuonyi, Voices of the Rio Grande* (anthology), *Waterways,* Wingbow Press,
White Pine Press, *World's Edge* (Japan), *World Poetry* (Madras), Yoo-Hoo Press, *Zero.*

To my extended family, thanks for your patience, swift kicks, & support over the years.
Special acknowledgement: Arthur Sze, Scott Nicolay (advice, editing); Jeff Bryan (saké, pix-
els); Elaine LaMattina, Dennis Maloney (midwives). Gioia Tama, Jacquie Bellon (heart);
Harold Littlebird (song); Susan Heldfond (insight); Steve Sanfield (wild axe); David & Tina
Meltzer, Jack Hirschman, Melissa Mytinger (who lit the fuse) & Cecilia Woloch (for Paris,
which begins the next book).

Publication of this book was made possible, in part, by grants from
the National Endowment for the Arts and the New York State Council on the Arts.

Cover design: Jeff Bryan

Book design: Elaine LaMattina

First printing, 1995.

Manufactured in the United States of America.

9 8 7 6 5 4 3 2 1

Published by
White Pine Press
10 Village Square, Fredonia, NY 14063

To Giovanna & Joaquin—
Raise the cup, pass the flame,
Let the circle widen, the song extend!

Contents

Introduction /13

From *Desde Alla* (1971) & *Early Poems* (1966–68)

    Pascua / 21
    Chuquiribamba, Vernal Tide / 32
    Mascara on the Insomniac's Eye / 34
    Good Friday Poem / 37
    Morning in San Cristobal / 41
    Toluca Chrysler Car / 42

From *Emptylots* (1971)

    Untitled Venice / 47

From *Field Notes From Alaska* (1971)

    Poem from the Sanitary Fill / 53
    America End of the Worker's Season / 54

From *Looking For Minerals* (1975)

    It is Spring Now / 59
    From the Seat of a Farmall Super A Tractor / 60
    Smoke / 61
    Looking for Minerals / 62
    A Night in Early Autumn / 63
    It Will Get to be Ten Below / 64
    Searching for Owls on a Snowy Eve / 65

From *Andean Town Circa 1980* (1978)

    Andean Town Circa 1980 / 69
    Photographic Attempt, San Roque Market / 70
    Guayaquil - July 22 / 71
    Conch Diggers on the Esmeraldas Coast / 72
    Examination of the Old / 73
    Time Exposure, Downriver / 74
    A Cathedral in Quito / 75

Sacha Runa Fiesta / 76

From *Rite for the Beautification of All Beings* (1983)

Rite for the Beautification of All Beings / 81

From *Poems at the Edge of Day* (1984)

Poems at the Edge of Day / 89
We Speak to What is Blossoming / 90
Song for Eve / 91
That Which Offers Itself / 92
For a Girl on the Beach of Seven Towers / 93
It is a Long Time Since I Have Asked / 94
Homage to Fire Which Quenches All Thirst / 95
To You O Goddess O Light / 96
For Radha, Nightfall / 97
Monkeys Know / 98
Our Geography is Heartbeat / 99

From *That Back Road In: Selected Poems 1972–83* (1985)

If They Ask / 103
These Places, Following Over / 104
At Mesa Verde / 105
The Woman Who Danced into Heaven / 107
Some Reasons for the Gods / 108
Angel Peak Overlook: A Road Song / 110
Gods Eyes for Sale / 111
From Desert Journals - 1975 / 113
No Matter What Road I Travel / 115
Homegoing, After Joaquin's Birth / 117
Turning Thirty Poem / 118
Poem, First Day of Summer / 121
Thankyou Joaquin, 7th Birthday / 122
Prayer at the Bend of a River / 125
A Song for October / 126
Winter Poem / 127
A Poem for the New Year / 128

From *Hymn for a Night Feast: Poems 1979–86* (1988)

Hymn for a Night Feast / 133
Woman Finding Herself / 134
These Things Tell Me to Remember You / 135
They'll Say You're on the Wrong Road / 137
A Poem for Green / 138
Faces Reflecting in Ink / 139
What Rite Had She? / 141
Reading *Ghost Tantras* / 143
Biting the Chill / 145
Preparing The Nets At New Stuyahok / 147
Aleknagik / 148
1+1+1+1+1+1=1 / 149
Madrigal, an April Morn / 151
Here, Give Me Your Hand / 152
It Is Not the You / 153
Rasa Lila, Kanchipuram / 155
I Am Not Thinking Anything / 156
Old Beast Self / 157
A Message from Han Shan / 160
True Love / 162
A Poem for Light / 164

From *Shadow Play: Poems 1987–91* (1992)

Shadow Play / 173
I See You in a Dream / 174
This Language Isn't Speech / 177
I Saw Kit Carson Still Alive / 179
At Wovoka's Ghostdance Place / 182
To a Young Student, Blizzard Hill / 183
North Country, a Sketch / 185
For Hasya / 186
Threnody for Chama Ruiz / 187
The Body Burns Strong / 188
To the Burmese Military Regime / 189
Fragments from Insomnia / 191
Lyric Written With Both Hands / 192
This Poem for Maria Still Inside / 193
Journal Entry, West of Reno / 195
About to Title a Painting for a Friend / 198
Field Guide to the Body's Anatomy / 199
Song of the Talus / 201
Prologue in the Key of C / 203

To the Angel Half Fire Half Snow / 204
Two Bodies / 205
For This We Come / 206
A Song for Autumn / 207

New Poems (1991–1994)

Sending Out The Ghosts / 211
Natural History of a Whitened Landscape / 212
From Desert Journals / 213
E Train to Spring from Port Authority / 214
Listen, The Promise is Hidden / 220
Of Energy, Ebony, Rosewater & Lime / 221
From Himal Journal / 225
Guess, Feel, Doubt, Brighten the Air / 228
I Forgot Myself Last Night / 230
No Superlatives Please / 232
I Reconstruct Her as I Touch / 235
Turning Fifty Poem / 238

HEARTBEAT GEOGRAPHY

INTRODUCTION

1·6·94:
EPIPHANY:
Jemez
N.M.

years unravel
winepress tightens
tales keep balance
wings fold
Eyeli grows younger
Bounty flows
ecstasies
hieghten
their wave. ♪

NORTH
out through
Spirit Sings
portals in its
landscape made
wherever Tracked,
alphabeta planted
where I stand,
Home is exactly

Below me,
the Dream Maze
Above me,
the Dream Maze
& between;
a Mirror
of glistening
Sand;
topography bathed
in Rosy Fluorescence
becoming
Sacred Braille
read with Foot

Heat waves
in Dancing
full of windows
the journey
Trance-Lucent,
Body through Body
Sole-full See,
Sail their
Ships
Relation

The Word, the Flesh, and John Brandi

A weekly newsmagazine tells me that scientists have identified the chemical con-
stituents of love in the human body. For some, I know this might be unwelcome
news, another example of science gone too far. But I am thrilled to find evidence
that supports another understanding — that love is part of a complex system, pro-
foundly linked to the body; that the body and soul are one, at least for awhile. A few
weeks later, John Brandi sends me a passage from his journal, written in Juneau,
Alaska in 1968, at a time when he was keeping one step ahead of the draft board:

> "I am convinced now
> that the poem is Liquid, it is
> manufactured in the Body,
> not in the Brain—"

He claims no particular reason for sending that note, but I include it as a rare and
luminescent statement of a poetics that is never — not even in this case — mani-
fested outside of the poetry which it inhabits. As such, it reveals the primary impor-
tance of the flesh in Brandi's poetry — flesh not in the negative protestant sense of
the word, but in the way which I tried to touch on briefly above, the sense of a flesh
which is never separate from the soul itself, whose every secretion is entirely sacred.
And among these secretions then let us number poetry and love; indeed, I hope
many of us would number them as one.

I like to think that this is close to what Fenollosa intended when he wrote "Poetry
agrees with science and not with logic." This because true science is no more a
product of logic and the intellect than true poetry. At their best, both are based on
long and careful observation of the world charged with the most direct intuition. It
is only the scientist or the poet who would lie in the grass for hours to watch an
insect cross a leaf. To do so is a kind of love.

So then let us have the outline of an alchemical equation which draws together
love and poetry, body and soul, then retrieves science from the intellect in order to
begin the mapping of one of the more energetic and physical poetries presently
being written.

The flesh is the starting point, the reason why when reading Brandi's poetry I am
often reminded of Jeff Goldblum's line in The Fly: "You've got to be crazy for the
flesh." Brandi is, and in the most positive way, like old Walt Whitman enthralled by
the sight of healthy men and women at work (those who dismiss Whitman's inter-

est as entirely sexual, miss the point, since it goes far beyond that). It is what has long been most lacking from European and American poetry, and only begins to re-emerge with Whitman, Melville, Rimbaud, Lorca, Neruda (it is there too, in Emily Dickinson, ominously — "the loaded gun," as Susan Howe points out, is the poet's own body). But halfway through this century, it is an awareness still so desperately needed that Olson must write, "knives, anything, to get the body in."

Brandi does get the body in, and there are knives sometimes: "The dictator cuts apart geography/on his human meatboard." Although he does not celebrate the cruel, the violent, the grotesque, he does not turn away from them either. When he sees them, he reports them unflinchingly, in poems all the way from the early "Pascua" to the more recent "To the Burmese Military Regime" and "I Saw Kit Carson Still Alive." It is as often from here in the United States as abroad that the experiences that give birth to these poems come. When they do come, Brandi accepts them, turns his light on them, turns them into poetry. And what he celebrates in these poems is the continuance, the survival, of the human spirit, through all cruelty and torture. There is much that is political here, but nothing doctrinaire; it is the poetry of someone who, having been to these places and known the people there, cannot help, if honest, to report what was seen. In this he recalls Rimbaud, allowing the drunken boat of his life to carry him where it will, even to hell, and the poetry itself evolves as the record of this journey. Brandi's own journey begins not on a drunken boat but on a drunken train, in a jungle like the one where Rimbaud's ended, his body rotting away from him.

Brandi knows that the vulnerability of the flesh cannot be escaped; in "Field Guide to the Body's Anatomy," he writes:

> "Flesh can be poked, pierced, cooked, penetrated
> asked for, given, received, tampered with, made sacred
> kept clean, stripped, dressed, masked, moved
> kidnapped, stored, held in ransom, given a price."

But the flesh is much more than the sum of its weaknesses. It is the dual potential of the flesh, for both suffering and sacredness (the latter even arising from the former) that most concerns Brandi: body is link with Earth and heaven — the same poem also says: "Veins branch from arteries like Bombay streets/Shoulders once had wings." This is not the only place Brandi suggests that the identity of body with soul predates this life; in the poem from which this volume's title derives, he writes: "We all begin/as mirrors, naked/with bodies once solar/begetting form." Brandi's poetry gathers and accumulates the music which celebrates the body in all its weakness and holiness, generating a sense of blessing, of ceremony, which is often made explicit, as in "Rite for the Purification of All Beings," at the end of which he writes: "I speak with blood & motion beyond language."

The physical is further manifested in the world itself, from which even the Bible admits the flesh arose. Brandi embraces the world with an unrestrained passion, celebrating it in sexual terms. Neruda is certainly a model in this, but where Neruda saw a landscape in the lover's body, Brandi sees a lover's body in the landscape. This becomes clear in many of his wonderful glyph-poems, as breasts and vulvas emerge in a landscape others term barren, but which he clearly loves.

Brandi draws himself across the world, making love to it through his poetry as he goes. The poems, he writes in a letter, are "a report on the life . . . a road map of/witnessing/inner/outer/geographies." Geographically, this map begins in the Ecuadorian Andes during a Peace Corps stint over a quarter of a century ago. "Pascua" is the first poem from this period, and thus begins the book. It is the record of the author's attendance at one of the many wondrous syncretistic rituals of the Americas, where the indigenous cultures of the Americas meet the West everyday and scholars hardly notice. The scenes he encountered were "too intense or surreal to alter." Reading his descriptions of the activity on the packed Easter train, one is reminded of Charles Olson in Yucatan riding a bus crowded with Mayan people, and realizing that "they wear the flesh differently." For Olson, this was the beginning of his awareness of the need to reintroduce the physical into poetry. For Brandi, it is the discovery of purpose, of an unfiltered connection to a world which must be put down in writing. "It is my task," he writes in another poem from the same period, "to serve the original color of things, the tainted/circumstance of things, the un-Wordsworthian field of things." Here is the emergence of a social consciousness which will be an important part of all the work to follow.

From there the journey continues, as Brandi fled the draft, through California (Venice), Canada, Alaska, Mexico, and finally, after being cleared, to a home in New Mexico. It is here that he found "an internal geography/where man, animals, elements, & Oversoul all come to terms." Many more journeys follow, to South America, India, the Himalayas, Bali, and always Mexico, and many wonderful poems record them all. Not only in this relentless and ecstatic journeying, but also through the unrestrained breath of his early poems and the scrupulous honesty with which he reports the true nature of his experience, Brandi recalls Kerouac, his most immediate predecessor. I remember a conversation with Eliot Weinberger, that very fine translator of Paz and Huidobro, wherein he complained (referring to a currently popular school of poetry) that "poets today don't go anywhere." Brandi does, and brings eloquent record always. He is one of the few poets writing in English who has a clear concept of this hemisphere's geography and poetic tradition beyond that language.

The life that Brandi "reports on" is a life so closely intermingled with its surroundings that the cycles of the Earth come to be his own. He follows the seasons like the Japanese hokku poets, letting his verse swell and contract with the mood of the Earth. The milestones of the road and the milestones of his life then become a counterpart to the movements of the season cycle, as in the "Turning 30," and "50" poems. "Tonight,/I am fifty years old/watching the wheel go round." Flesh moves through world, world moves through flesh. Eventually, he seems to say, if he comes perfectly into harmony with the world's rhythms, the oneness of world and flesh will be completely enacted, and the poet will, like Han Shan, return "to the very Center/leaving no trace of himself/between highrock cliffs." And it is through the celebration of the sacred in the physical that such a return becomes possible.

World and flesh then are but two bodies the poet can inhabit. Coming into sync with his surroundings, the poet acquires a new way of seeing, as in the poem "Gods Eyes For Sale." And that is the role that Brandi has found for himself, as spokesperson for a magical world, which gives him its eyes in exchange for his mouth, his hand. Although my title's allusion casts Brandi in the role of devil, there are no devils here; what evil is shown is always human, and carries with it thus the hope of redemption. Brandi himself is more of a trickster, dancing in defiance of the destroyers wherever they appear. Where his feet touch the ground, a poem remains. Through the poem, he vanishes into and re-emerges from the Earth endlessly.

The combined vision of the flesh and the world it inhabits is only the beginning, for it is from this combination that the sacred emerges: "outside the self/lives another One of us, who conducts/the world with a spiral wand." Our souls and the world's soul merge. This knowlege is a gate "that can be locked/or unlocked forever/among us all."

A few months ago, while sprawled out in my living room with Brandi's poems all around me in the process of helping edit this volume, I drifted off and had a strange and telling dream. I was watching a huge globe of the world, spinning in front of me, and began to see it through the lens of Brandi's poetry. Suddenly its surface was transformed from rock and water to a skin of many-hued flesh, very alive, and peppered with the odd little icons of Brandi's glyph-poems, grown three-dimensional in the manner of monopoly tokens. This is the journey that this book offers, a trip through a world whose flesh is warm, whose heartbeat you can hear, here in the rhythms of John Brandi's poetry. "And you/are invited/into the house, the poem/the blood, the wheel. . ."

— Scott Nicolay
Farmington, New Mexico

I

from
DESDE ALLA
(1971)
&
EARLY POEMS
(1966-68)

...and this Clown of a Man is Me.; this poem of a face & Body, mine.. ~these Bones attached to Spine: musical Ladders of stick & marrow inside a Cloth Hymnal of Flesh fading & Transient in the Rags of shortening years...as the Days, ...Hours, Minutes go Loco from the ice-WIND of my BALCONY ~

J:67

Pascua

I. *In Riobamba*

There was the long shrill of the whistle
in the train station as the sun tried to make it through
the clouds, gray skies, first sights of Easter Sunday in Riobamba,
Christ already having risen, drunks staggering in threes
bouncing off gargoyles, bouncing off the door
of the Almacén Jaqueline, down Calle Larrea
singing: *Vamos a comer vamos a comer*
                vamos a comer a comer

The naked figure of myself as I stood looking at it
in the morning wind, feet ice cold on the cement balcony
of a friend's apartment, music still spinning from
last night: Debussy — Images: her body in a Guatemalan blanket
stained with sweet brown wine, still sleepy
propped against the wall wearing my souvenir corduroy cap.
I threw my jacket over her. The tape spun off:
the music we turned on to last night.
In the next room Miguel slept soundly; the air was thick
and full of tobacco.
The evangelists assembled in the park and began with off-tune
gospel songs, but Christ had already risen
and there was no sunrise.

I went back to feel her; to see that she was still there.
Pulled her face into mine, let my hands drop
into her, saw her eyelids open and laugh.
A book by Arthur Rimbaud lay opened on the table, singing
of phosphors waking yellow and blue.
An oily paper sack was crumpled on the floor; last night
we ate fresh bread with honey and butter.
Today the taste is still in my mouth.
I got up to close the door on the evangelists in the park:

"True I have wept too much! Dawns are heartbreaking;
  Cruel all moons and bitter the suns.
  Drunk with love's acrid torpors,
  O let my keel burst! Let me go to the sea!"

But Christ had already risen and there was no sunrise.

Of last night I had no remembrance.
When I was dressed, I stood with her by the wrinkled glass
window listening to Gregorian chants — and pulled her against me.
The chimes rattled in the cathedrals down the street;
against the window her hair and eyes blended into the sky.
The glass became moist with our breath; I drew a cross in it.
In the park the evangelists kept on singing.
The second time, when the whistle blew, I was gone.

II. *To Columbe*

Outside on the corner
Dalia slept next to her mother's fruit stand: a green wooden cart
with iron-spoked wheels pushed to a stop in the wet pavement.
A light canvas cloth covered apples, pears and mandarins.
The bananas were rotting.
Dalia slept in a man's gray overcoat on the curb next to the cart.
When I passed she seemed to have given me a mandarin
— and I took it.
Yet, when I turned back to look, she was still asleep.

The train was pulling out of town chugging black smoke
as the sun tried to make it through the clouds.
Many passengers were going down the line to Columbe;
the cars were full. When they added more second-class coaches
I was seated next to an old farmer who claimed there was gold
on his farm, that last night he had seen blue flames
glowing above a broken bush. Across the aisle was a couple
still in youth: she was a curly-headed girl snuggled
up against her mate; he wore a spattered painter's cap,
dark suit and tan oxfords.

The women came through in checkered aprons,
carrying enameled pans of hot potatoes and rings of onions;
they carried buckets of warm milk with yellow cream floating on top
and waxed paper with handfuls of steaming broadbeans.
Most of the passengers sat facing each other on wooden benches
and stared out the opposite windows, beyond each other's faces.
It was still early, Christ had already risen
and there was no sunrise.

Outside Riobamba we passed the roundhouse
and the unfinished church at Licán.
Near Cajabamba workmen in ragged jackets conversed
at the side of the track, their red flags dropped into the black ash
next to the wheels of a handcar. The shadow of smoke passed
over the men and fell on ripening fields of wheat.
We were taking on water in Cajabamba when a frightened
Indian woman with baby tried to board the train.
No one let her through — and she got off.
Somebody remarked:
  "Vé a la mujer, Mister. ¿Qué le parece?
  Three thousand Indians here.
  We have to keep them in order, no?"
Going up the grade to Balbanera I rode on the outside
of the coach. Dust and cinders covered my forty-Sucre jacket.
We passed the lagoon and the old hacienda house at Colta.
Blue haze hung on the lake, crows flew away into the distance
dipping low over tilted scarecrows.
Inside me I remembered all the places to where they flew:
 to Lirio
   and Huayallalo and Cebollar,
and further — where only the *páramo* grew.
We passed San Antonio and La Merced.
Along the road the Indians were all going in the one direction:
to Columbe. Where Christ had risen.

III. *Columbe*

I lost my mind as soon as the train pulled into
the green station and we unloaded: Indians and whites
poured out of the coaches and from inside boxcars
and from the tops: men, women, children
animals, baskets, ponchos: a mass of color and noise
leaving the train lopsided on the track. Startled conductors
against empty brown windows. Engineer and fireman
in the cast-iron black locomotura — a hand raised
grabbing the whistle chain — a long scream of revenge
as the train creaks out of town
     down the narrow-gauge tracks.

Columbe was shoved up against a lifeless
chalk hill with earthen homes and uneven mud walls

and a whitewashed church with an empty plaza surrounded
by crumbling tiendas. The faded village grew
from a hallucinogenic splash of Indians spread
through narrow streets like a flood of drunken lava:
a surreal clash of yellows, veridians, reds, violets, blacks,
oranges, prussians, indigos, vermilions, and snow white.
They dripped over the walls like flowers.
My mind ripped open and spilled out.
Twisted and bleating tinpan bands sounded at every corner.
Groups of Indians from backland hamlets marched
in wild costumes, drinking trago and chicha, spitting
inside their horns, flashing rusty swords, pounding wooden drums;
saluting flowers and cactus; lining mud walls in drunken frenzy
to curtsy the white townsfolk. Some wore ancient military uniforms,
patched and sewn-over hundreds of times;
some had insane polka-dot ties from the Thirties, layers of spotted
and checkered shirts, rubbertire shoes, goggles, green visors,
gasmasks, mayordomos' hats. Others hid behind thick sunglasses,
raising bouquets of paper flowers, heads wrapped in persimmon
and sap-green scarves, bodies draped in soiled banners
— red, yellow, and black — shot full of holes
by muzzle-loading rifles fed with steelball ammunition.

The Indians assembled: band members,
wives and children of band members, leaders of bands,
guardians, directors, acrobats and intoxicated promotion men.
One blast after another; chilling screeches rising
from coronets and trumpets and battered French horns;
jangling brass bells; broken tambourines: smoking cymbals, wood flutes
and German-made harmonicas dripping with saliva:
each wiry orchestra out of its mind drunk
trying to outdo each other
up the steps of the temple to play for the emancipated Spirit
of Christ over his great decaying altar.

— the rich bastard *patrón* weaving through the crowd
   pushing away Indian women, stopping to piss against a fallen
   trumpet player rolled in the street; the boss man, in full view,
   dribbling urine down his brown leather boots
                          and his heavy wooden cane.

And the white village people
serving barrel after barrel of chicha spiked with ammonia
to the masked Indian serfs: taking every bit of little change
from the boiling multitude, piling the stinking silver in back rooms.
And the church officials
wringing money and food from rolled-up handkerchieves
and cheap leather purses tied beneath the flaming
skirts of the farmers' wives.

Then another out-of-key screaming-drunk tin trio
trying to make it up the steps of Christ's tabernacle, pushed
and beaten away by the acolytes and daughters of the whites.
Sound of gunfire and powder and sparks
into the gray sky where Christ had already risen.
Men kissing, hugging, saluting, dancing with other men.
Societies of make-believe *junta militares* in crooked tan army caps,
metal war bonnets, aluminum St. Christopher medals,
fluorescent capes pinned with cast-iron cows, sheep, eyes
hips, lungs, martyrs, virgins, saints, pigs and donkeys.
Cardboard shields pinned with glass jewels,
splintered mirrors, yellow beads, cobalt sequins, cloth hymnals
from the missions, flattened aluminum pieplates from Quito
dumpsters, used dentures from the Ambato market.

— a drunk crazy Indian standing in an erect knot,
    puffed cheeks, jiggling body, spasmodically blowing
    into a bent brass horn.

— and sound of more horns, more blasts of shrill notes
    more bands trying to make it up Christ's altar
    more gunshots hitting dust and walls
    and void sunless air: more clash of color and bodies
    floating downhill like warm juice from an exploded volcano.
    More money being collected for the Holy Mass.

— the high priest casually dresses himself
    in flowing white vestments, crosses himself several times
    and ties his cincture.

IV. *Offering of the Mass*

I was wedged into a sod hut
with cold soaking floors where men and women
lifted bowls and tumblers to their faces
and alcohol spilled down their amber cheeks;
where women fell to the floor with runny-nosed babies
in salmon-colored bonnets, and men
became polluted and crumpled over and fell
on the babies and women — eyes wide open
straight to the ceiling, while

Down on the square the multitude continued to drink
the whites continued to take in money
the church officials continued to collect fees
the Indian bandleaders waved their orchestras up the rock steps
to Christ's altar: the awful cacophony of noise and injustice
repeated itself over and over: repeated itself
in the gunshots and wounds
in the piled high money
in the slobbering mouths
in the high priest in the plaza chanting the Mass
inside a thick pall of incense and fumes.

I was walking down a hill through the orgasm
of men and women trying to see the bald-headed master
bring into view the great risen Christ; trying to see the great *brujo*
fill himself with wine, his pockets jingling with the aluminum
Sucres of the poor as he raised the unleavened bread
of crucified Christ's body over the intoxicated crowd:
the tin soldiers, the chapped brides, the wrinkled grandmothers,
the cloudy-eyed *taitas*, the crack-lipped kids, the blind
albinos — who were for years cast under the feudal yoke
of the whites; who were every day of every year made to serve
as caged-in animals on the eroded haciendas, and who had been let out
this one Sunday to once again be taken advantage of by the whites,
began to mock their national army, began to mock
from the very start the politics they never had a say in,
the society they never got a chance at,
the education which had been prohibited them for at least
four-hundred years — the Indians, the tin soldiers, the mock armies
and mock societies and eyeshade presidents in slouched

cranberry-colored caps now began to jiggle
and puff into their shrieking horns and wail on their brass flutes.
Drunken platoons loaded and fired their rifles.

Fired into the ground and fired into the sky.
Shot off the wooden arm of the ragged-haired virgin
dressed in pink and brown satins.
Shot off the thorns of icon-Christ and shot off
his head. Ripped open his chest with gunfire.
While the high priest remained chanting, and the Altar Society
officials took up another collection, and the so-called
upper-caste village merchants continued to pour liquor
down the throats of the Indians.

— a glassy-eyed peasant turns up his transistor radio
    full blast and listens to his own song.

And the splintery thorns of Jesus Christ that morning
in Columbe, like every other Easter Sunday
these beaten-down human beings had ever known,
had fallen from the wooden deity unnoticed
into the head of a drunken man asleep between the legs
of his wife while someone's baby crawled
for her breast, and again like four centuries ago
the mother was knocked out, her eyes wide open to the
gray sky where the Savior had already risen.
And around this intoxicated holy family, around this Mary
Joseph and Christ child, the last of the standing bands wound itself up
and marched around them; the last of the clear white liquor
was emptied from a Coke bottle. Around their faces
it burned with a silent flame.

I was walking away from it all when I saw
an Indian woman not drunk, but singing a low melody to her child:
she stood in velvet green robes with a long white apron,
the child on her back. Dust swirled into her eyes, into
her straight black hair, up through the squirming foetus
concealed in the pregnant stomach.
Smoke from dying incense blurred her face.
She chanted a mournful *carnaval* song to her child.
She recalled her grandparents who lived on the high pampa.
She recalled how no sun had come with the dawn

of that morning — Easter Sunday
at least four centuries ago.

She left with gunfire dancing about her,
through the streets of Columbe where Christ had risen.
She left as they strung up a living icon on a platform
with steel cables under wreaths of eucalyptus and pine.
At the feet of this enthroned child-lady they threw black petals
and paraded the armless statue of the Holy Virgin Mother.

— the priest finished chanting once and for all,
    disrobed himself, and settled into his renaissance chair.
    He drank Johnnie Walker. Expensive stuff. Imported.

— the vendors walked among the fallen troops,
    looked for life here and there, came like scavenger birds
    to pickpocket the dead, sold pastries of the Sacred Heart
            to the living.

— and when the first women began to come about from
    their drunken sleep, they examined their men,
    smelled the vomit and excrement on the soil — heard
    the snickering whites go back to their houses and stores
            and from under their blouses they took a few
    cold potatoes, forced the men to eat,
            and fed the babies.

It was a scene after a battle. Broken bodies, defeated
soldiers, mock presidents, twisted tin armies lay scattered in dung
and glass. Wives and daughters wept above hemorrhaging faces
wrapped in torn banners.

V. *Return*

When the afternoon whistle blew
at the station in Columbe, I was leaving.
The engine chuffed; carriages jerked at their couplings.
The landscape out the window, past the brakeman's legs,
froze in my mind.
I looked back at the town where Christ had risen.
I looked in the coach again — and forgot.

Near the watercloset, a brass spigot dripped with rust.
Urine trickled under the door and down the aisle. The train
jumped back and forth across the loose rails: a few Indians slept
by the open windows, the soiled ribbons on their pressed-wool hats
fluttered out into the air and strobed the landscape.

A cock flapped its wings at the bottom of my feet
under the seat. There were cherries wrapped in a plastic bag
crushed on the floor. And cheese wrapped
in an old newspaper soaked with urine from the leaking
watercloset. A slow mauve light broke from the clouds
and spread across the varnished forehead of a fat woman,
her swollen belly covered by a wool blanket.
A child put down an apple, half eaten.
It rolled into a corner — and turned brown.

A vendor nudged my arm with his tray of sweets
and salted biscuits. He wore a dark suit with orange stripes, dirty
where it had rubbed against the outside of the train.
I could not escape the vendor. I could not escape the inside
of the coach. I could not escape the odors of men and women
and babies, the piled-high suitcases warped and battered;
the cloth bags of rotten fruit, the smell of fresh newspaper ink
from the first-class coach; corn cobs on the floor,
lemon peelings and pineapples rolling between dried fish;
tea in muslin; gunnysacks of fowl; crates of cabbages
where drunks rested their perspiring heads.

In first class, businessmen dusted
pin-striped suits and covered their mouths
with embroidered handkerchieves to escape the *'mal aire.'*
Wives with puffed hair, ointments and spray, fragrance of brandy
and geranium, kept their eyes closed — brushed dandruff
from Easter outfits. The conductor told a dirty joke
The local *hacendado* in checkered riding pants and cardigan wool
tapped his steel-tipped shoes, and laughed.
People from the coast. People from the cities.
Tourists tossing coins out the windows to poor villagers
of the pampa, snapping photos of Easter Sunday
morning, saying:

   "Vé a la mujer. Vé al Indiocito.

¡Vé a ese payaso!"

But,

"Christ rose! Christ rose!" I say in my mind.
Train wheels click. Whistle tears open its throat and blows.
Train wheels click. Train wheels
click. Train wheels click . . .

— nothing stops to hear anybody around here.

Women stagger in the swirling landscape,
sky is still gray, sun lights up the herds of sheep for a moment.
Shepherds hold out their hats and bow to the train,
animals pass with blue flames over their backs.
A man in sheepskin trousers falls flat at the tracks, eyes
popped open like a corpse.

VI.

"Howling underneath the leaves
  The wolf spits out the lovely plumes
  Of his feast of fowls:
  Like him I am consumed."

Of last night, of times before, of that which
has already explained itself, I want no remembrance.

Now, in the plain a lonely horn bleats.
A tambourine jingles. Women struggle to hold up their men.
An amber face swirls in dust and incense: whistles shout,
boys play panpipes. All over, the landscape
is deep green and white: gray skyscape retreats
into fine mist; barley fields are hidden.
Heads pop from a bean patch, a tin drum rattles in the corn,
crows take flight over the grain, climb with frost
on their wings into the heights
                    — disappear into the sky.

Train approaches a black water tower
and stops.
Brakeman dips his flag.

A lantern flashes from the locomotive. Steam blows
into rain. My mind cannot think
now:

Christ has already risen. There was no sunrise.

Riobamba, Ecuador, 1967
(with lines from Rimbaud)

Chuquiribamba, Vernal Tide

There is no going on, only leaving off.
This, what-is-here-before-me, this must not be translated
into anything else other than what is:

Quaggy slump of pasture
bordered by wind-whirled stalks of flaming eucalyptus
blackly splaying the lemon-yellow air. And,
over there, suddenly in line of vision, a young but already bent
woman pounding laundry — the village priest's garments —
in the brown swirls of a polluted creek.

Here is the sunlit nape of her neck. Muddied calves,
reddened forearms, bronze chest, imperfect teeth lining
the partway open mouth. This, the Is of Her,
undreamed, imperfectly composed moment of labor
among squares of cloth on flattened flowers. This,
the slap-slap-rinse of working hands with head whose jet-black eyes
occasionally search skyward to un-ponder, re-dream, un-join
herself from the eroded volcanism of the landlord's
greed-divided hillside — No, this woman
must not be made into poetry, She whose very presence
is verse, is pain, is sorry goosebumped upper arms
and reddened fingers ringing not bells, but wringing iridescent
bubbles from twists of knotted robes and satin vestments,
she whose buttocks the color of clay bleed through
cheap sewn-together manufactured cottons
printed with import rural scenes, She whose singing
murmurs me out of place and ashamed, spying on her nymph-like
figure not 'nymph' at all, but — hardened, those calloused eyelids,
those crusty nipples on breasts wetly slapping the body
in back-and-forth rhythm of pure mountain light,
or—more accurately spoken when viewed again — *impure* eroded light
falling in jagged needles on rainless bumps of pasture where
one skinny lamb plays frightenedly in the agitated heat of noon.
Little symbolic lamb, whose fleece-branded dirty-wool right side
smolders with make-believe P A X sign — Lamb of Yahweh,
Lamb of reincarnate Joan of Arc whose half-shut eyes drip coagulated
mucus gathered by the poor to soothe their sores.

God willing, it is my task, then
to serve the original color of things, the tainted
circumstance of things, the un-Wordsworthian field of things,
the splintered and bleeding blotch of triangle darkening the center
of her dress, the stitched-together patches of cloth
juxtaposed with shining Taita Cura silk of things,
in the river and in the mind (little particles of thought)
or oozing between the feet (chaff, dust, wing) . . .
these things of rye and unidentifiable wilted stalks that struggle to grow
into eatable seed for the household of this young woman
certainly already mother of five, but — as in most cases — things
that won't be harvested for her at all
but for the stubble-whiskered patrón who landholds from
a far distance gluttoning it up in his city castle, properly dressed
forever cheating on his wife with that politically-erect thing
between his legs resembling the blunt sword of
ancestral, armored colonizer.

Which is what this is all about, which is why
wine-stains don't wash from Taita Cura's garments, or
the dusty, slapping breasts on the young woman's body
don't supplement her youngest child over there in the brown box
in the rushes — that crusty thing of a child who reaches
for torn sky between knotted snakes of dirty laundry.

I see her now, see myself out of focus
under the orb of heaven-to-come, within the Nada of now, the buzz
of hovering insects, the mad edge of black wind yellowing
the parchment hills, the reverse process of plants unseeding themselves
in the no-come-rain of destiny manifest not by land nor altitude nor lack
of cloud as much as by the Cura himself, the bloodline of serf and patrón,
the hell-torn pious master of worldy exile, all of it!
    — the What Is of this what-is-before-me, the now of Nada,
the Nada of myself bursting inside the iridescent bubble wrung from
that half-knotted article of existence below the chaffed arms,
the swinging crucifix, the milkless breasts of this
        un-iconized, should-be-canonized,
exactly there before me
                laboring woman.

Ecuador, 1966

33

Mascara on the Insomniac's Eye

I ask of you Father
a dusky feather in my powerless cap.
And Mother, wherever you aren't
I hope you fill me, put a stone in my mouth
rather than a lie, an unmortgaged star
to wet my impotence.

Today I won't read the bookmark between
Shakespeare or the spit mark on the overleaf
of the Bible, but will find the eroded secret
between the injustice in the eyes of night, will find
the reason behind the centuries of rain
that never make green this petrified land.

The National Palace is two blocks away
through the darkness under the dead moon
out the window . . .
A naked family in the Consul's alley
huddles in the half dawn, a religious
portrait gilded with repeated light . . .

But the fantasy is mine.
No flowery skin; no halos surround.
Just injured feet and faces,
lumped more like half-used firewood.

And this poem, not of me
nor yours, is given fire on the branch
by each and all of us — undeniably we have
created them as they have us.
The moon in the well, the sword in the martyr's chest,
the silver jag bloodying the carp's eye,
the satyr's hairy thrust, the vulture's thermal rise
with lizard in beak, the calf at the teats of her mother
and the dirty foam in war's wake — ours.

A swarm of bees invades my sleep.
The cherry tree flutters its magnetic leaves
as the world flames in symbolic dream.
You and I are caught

in the perfume abyss, in the carnival alley.
Black fire darts from guitar mouths,
black fire fills your kiss.
It's nearly 6 A.M. and intoxicated fools
trace their names on broken cobble while guards change
and police assemble and sweepers lift and let fall
their musical, ragged brooms.

It rained all night through the open window.
It's raining now as you walk backwards from the bed,
sun rising between your legs, lighting the wings
of your sex — your dark tree singing its birds of justice
back to the womb.   A moment — just a moment
posing unintentionally naked for me:
what sweet possibility,
this human Republic, what sea
of absolute spring might fill
        the mirror.

Quito: 25.XII.67

"I rise from the sheets and
look to Sea. I proclaim, like
Whitman proclaimed: eeI too
am come"

&
Know
in the shore-washed excess
of Joy & smiling Sorrow:
the poem is Liquid, it is
manufactured in the BODY
not in the Brain!

Good Friday Poem

I am caught undecided where to go confused inside
this muggy bus waiting to reach a religious desire to speak
the language of God the Father God the Son on the Cross
above the driver I am waiting for the image of the Savior
to come running down the streets between the bars & bus stations
& the tiendas I am waiting for Christ the Lord
to speak my language to shout his death on the front page
of the Tribune I am lost unable to come to an agreement
with the craving in my bones to satisfy the question that wanders
through my membrane I need to know if the agony of Christ
was in Gethsemane or in New Haven or in Cuzco or Naples or
Stalingrad or was it or is it or is it coming or is it everywhere
I think I know I think it's in that Coca Cola sign
Christ O hear me I see You dying everywhere
O Son O Father O Older than Confucius O Newer than Ford

*

I am caught undecided in the midst of a zone between
the neutral seas of knowing & not knowing
I hereby proclaim that from inside this bus I see
your bloody face beading up in the sweat on the backs
of the seated ladies I see the wood of your thorns wrapped
between the flowers around the trees I hear you mocked
in the policeman's whistle see your eyes in the intersection's
blinking caution light know you again in the old Pontiac's wobbling tire
I see your people seven of them crammed inside the doors
I catch you behind the wheel your pants hanging out the trunk
hands steadying the cross along the telephone-pole highway
to the outside of town — I see you dying everywhere
O Son O Father O Older than Confucius O Newer than Ford

*

I am caught undecided inside the S-shaped isthmus of Panama
looking up the sins of Mohammed feeling out the Hindu wants of man
craving the rebel saint of Buddha mentioning the old master of Tao
I am starting to dig the meaning in the suffering of the Chosen People
O Christ do you know I haven't the slightest idea of doing good nor bad
O Christ do you know I see you dying everywhere do you know

O Son O Father O Older than Confucius O Newer than Ford

*

You are the scorpion on the floor at my hotel room door
You are the serpent of the sea in ancient geography the sheep between
the cactus under the filter-tipped jet stopped in mid air
You are the beans between zigzag rows of barley the tilted huts
the flies at the wicks of lamps hoe of the peon whip of the mayordomo
coca between the raw gums of porters twelve thousand feet up
white wigs moss eyebrows leather ears masks on the faces
tails between the legs of prancing rocket men sequined ladies
in sperm-colored villages the echo of drums in rank alleys
blood of the swine on the Virgin's doorstep puta with her pan
on the floor by the springless bed after the Act of Consecration
pinetree onfire with the spark of a ceremony urine down the gutter
between the walls of the Citadel tightrope walker in the penny arcade
beggar chewing crusts off the cheesemaker's plate
a guy getting a haircut at Geronimo's nicked in the ear
It's you — I know you I see you everywhere
in the bleached plazas in the carnation stalls riding the broken oxcart
O Son O Father O Older than Confucius O Newer than Ford

*

You are north you are south you are east you are west
the downtown riot in the eleven o'clock news the wet cigarette
dangling from Tempest Storm's lower lip in her westside apartment
Christmas tree dying in the city dump perfume between the legs
of the Seventh Street clerk gargled hack from the unemployed no neck
in her make-believe skirt I see You tonight sleeping on broken bottles
I see you at dawn in your baggy t-shirt & busted loafers
sister of El Rey de los shoeshine boys brother whose father swallows
fire for the mannequin rich at the Gruta Azul spastic kid selling tongues
peeling fur from cow stomachs at the mercado central
You wipe blood from the tiles at Elvia's You sweep my feet by mistake
You bare your neon tits for fat-eyed cigar smokers at El Disco Quito
that's You in the burglar-alarm sunrise squatting to piss
under the boot heel of Pegasus that's You the rattle of crooked dice
the fires in Callao the fires of one-hundred-thousand world steel mills
that's You the blaze under the seats in the backrow of the Roxy
smoke from mud ovens of Mishongavi smoke from brick ovens at Auschwitz
smoke from Cambodia's torn eyelids smoke from the juice machines

blowing a fuse smoke from the lost tipis along the bottomland
of the Little Big Horn smoke from the crotch of the flannel man
at the rear entrance of the Beaver Patch — I see You
the junky the priest the burnt-out missionary dropping string beads
dropping Book of Mormon dropping paper Watchtower
through broken boardwalk where the girl with crepe wings hammers
orange-crate caskets where the mother of nine sweeps
bones collects hair wipes the slaughterhouse her pushcart fulla fruit
her pushcart fulla brains her pushcart fulla nails
for the teethless old lady Christs haggard in the nicotine breeze
for the haggard madwoman her clothes off dancing behind factory row
for the haggard young bride collating late-night bindery-shop Bibles
I see you once I see you twice I know you a third time
in the chemical laughter of public fountains in the broken church chime
in square-jawed lovers kissing at ChiChi's in the cock behind the zipper
pushed to one side in the snatch under the skirt burning
in the orphaned moves of parkbench domino men
in the commissioned hollers of wire-cage ticket vendors
in the electric saints blinking over the spittle-lipped kid feeding grandpa
a burntsienna coughdrop — & the whorechild brushes her teeth
with a dead twig — & the canary pecks out fortunes from a velvet curtain
strung with plastic milagros
You are this You are that You are the foetus in the angel
above the torn cloud dumping rock onto Huarás
dumping shit into the pearl diver dumping exhaust into Woolworth's Latino
I hear you I see you coming all the way from Puerto Montt
Antofagasta Bogotá Quetzaltenango Mérida Illiniza Sigsig Gila Bend Truth or
Consequences Old Oraibi Alcatraz Sand Creek & Tambopampa
You are rain into the basins rain off the synclines rain down the roofs
into sewers & charmboxes into coin machines onto the acolyte
with candle burning his hair under the Tenth Station of the Cross
I know You I see You dying everywhere

Yes

I am caught undecided confused on where to go I can't stand
another speech somewhere between birth control & the H bomb
napalm bodies glowing in Asian dark tell-it-like-it's-not history books
fat-nosed presidents handcuffing Peace troupes
I am sick of astrological figurings done with blow ups wards time zones
lookalike armies air-raid Vatican new hat new shoes political apeman
mafia spaceman colonial stars bigot stripes threat of World War III

stagnant countdowns oilslick breeze Bazooka Joe Diet Rite FBI USAID
I am saying Goodbye So Long to fumed cities deadbody ocean
sawmilled freewill popbottle assassination hit & run mental games
I am no longer concerned with whether they make the sex act
unprohibited the Moon free territory newsprint safe to eat I won't
raise flags sell slogans call mother on short wave trying to decide
whether to live north south east west of the Equator
knowing what to think of Good Friday

Yes
O Son O Father O Older than Confucius O Newer than Ford
I know You at last I know You I see you dying everywhere

Today

I was searching around in my head to see if I could remember You
being crucified coming down off your cross waking up from the tomb
going back to the manger with a little surprise ——————————

Local Draftboard
Canal Zone, 1968

Morning in San Cristobal

Sky bends and lowers
over tired, conquered Mexico.

In Love's cry, was it me, that ragged man
with one eye about to explode, that woman with clanking pails
limping between facades spiked with cast-iron fleur de lis
to keep out the thieves?

You remind me I loved you as an earthly thing,
your carnation a momentary throne.
And this struggle, these dusty labor laws piled before windows
finger-marked with uneven light, the warm bread
of each breast, the speckled tiger lily in the vase
and blood's taste on the tongue:

None have shore
for the Dove
to rest.

Pensión Dolores
San Cristobal, Chiapas

Toluca Chrysler Car Family

I.

Ya see the Chrysler there
Ya see the tailpipe battered heavy old Chrysler there

Ya see the early morning Toluca frost dotted crystals
on the backseat window. Ya see the bulwark of exhaust blackened
migration bug blood yellow sulfur mothed grill ornament

Ya see mileage worn warm hearted white haired
Mexican man check the tire tread on the left rear
Ya hear the darty eyed brown sandaled attendent man ask, "Lleno?"

Ya hear softly uttered reply voice of spare change
pocket recount, "No. Ten pesos, por favor."
Ya see first born straight faced passenger seat worn gray
scratchy armrest boy

Ya see second and third and fourth born on the road
insecticide haired leafy fingered Texas heat Arkansas cottonball
Denver slaughterhouse Georgia peachpicker arms and hands

Ya see mother and daughter farm bureau photo
look alike eyes nose mouth hair
Ya see daughter again; ya see cautious doubletake reglance
smile through hazy time burnt sun bubbled windshield

Ya see head of the family man gentle half worried
not go too fast we'll make it man lift foot over runningboard
throw in the clutch pedal spring in the ass
lumpy car seat press the ignition twice man

Ya hear the Chrysler car

Ya hear the Mexican man ask rolling down the window
in broken English, "Cuanto a California?"
Ya hear yourself in slowed down quiet utterance of reply,
"A week, tal vez cinco días — hittin it good"

II.

Ya see the car there
Ya see the Chrysler car there
Ya see the man and his family
Ya see them there
Ya smell the exhaust roar now . . .

Toluca-Altacomulco
Mexico

I don't even
take The candle
By The Handle,

I Live insted
with the Fingers
Directly around
the Flame

II.

from
EMPTYLOTS
(1971)

*"Make a picture of what you're frightened of
so you can master it."*
— Joan Miró

Untitled Venice

I am in Venice again
walking the canals to Jack's house
listening to Country Joe & The Fish on a pocket transistor
stopping at Alan's watching Richard Burton reruns
passing around a reefer eating a Sloppy Joe on Wonder Bread
looking over Mona Lisa looking over Cleopatra
with an Egyptian fan wrapped in towels in Hollywood
hopping a slow freight to Barstow
with Woody Guthrie in the Library of Congress
misplacing an offset Warhol litho of Marilyn Monroe
coughing on the smoke of a Fidel Castro cigar

I am Venice again
thinking over last winter in New York
bumped from Pan Am walking low-rent
in slow advance under river to Factory City
crosscountry redeyed through smokestack apocolypse
frisked by Virginia troopers   breath-pause at Fairy Springs
pissing in Sparta   riding a Batmobile out of Noster Nob
sick on canned stew in the Ozarks remembering a guy named Charlie
sharing pigmeat in a burntout housetrailer
reading over HOWL Frank O'Hara & Red Cats
backside of Mormon Temple bums on cardboard in Circleville
Moses under tablets in Orderville   sound asleep
fighting ghosts of genocide bottom of Cañon de Chelly
soaking my feet with a Senator's son
caught inside Bel Air dumpster
rolling tangerines into Pingileen's lap
paying off the cops naked in Bluebell's apartment
watching my face disintegrate in the bathroom mirror
hoping for a break in my life

I am in Venice again
walking away from popup sprinkler heads
ringing telephones longdistance hydraheads
arsenist brushfires Saniflush Old Spice Brut
& the Thing in 3-d   I am leaving plowed-under missions
tractored orange groves blood on North Hollywood draft files

47

perhaps they'll find me   issue a warrant
to prohibit me from leaving the country   jail me
end of the line nineteen hundred sixty eight
year of my twenty second birth day   dotdot dashdash dittoditto
shit of etceteras shiezze of mierdas caca of dada
popguns & paperweight time bombs
napalm orgies tinkertoy bigboys fat tie missionaries
bicycling up to gold doorknockers of old Mafia schoolmates
bragging along freeways with alias girlfriends   shortened lastnames
in smoking chrome monsters spraying ducktails squeezing tittie
throwing stag parties on Hong Kong yachts
ten degrees north of where my best buddy's
fighting for godknowswhat
waiting with his callgirl outside a tailorshop
sick with dysentery dead a few days later
whatthehell whatsthematterhere?
I PROTEST! as more bombs hit the news
as stocks take a rise &
GM builds another
surprise

I am in Venice again
still walking the canals to Jack's
letting loose bomb blast caught inside me
over Bikini Atoll over Hiroshima over Dresden in Saigon
another AP wirephooto of Buddha burning himself
another Breakfast of Champions president grooming himself
gogo girl in the Satin Doll drunk killed hit & run on Pico
another book on Jack Ruby Rolling Stones &
Dow Chemical

I am in Venice again
perhaps only to pack my bags & leave
walk out past sand foam & oilslick to be sucked cock ball & chain
down under away from obsolete earthmen
power fear machinery sex & negotiations
backrooms of Popes & politics
ye old Us

I am in Venice again
ready to take that refreshing walk into the sea
& sink out of sight into the mouth of Old Killer Whale
who waits with hellos from Jonah inside
his belly

Good bye —

Venice Wharf
22.II.68

III.

from
FIELD NOTES FROM ALASKA
(1971)

*"Keep track of every day
the date emblazoned in yr morning."*
— Jack Kerouac

11 Oct. 68
AUK BAY
Alaska:

DOS VISTAS de la Luz
Verde y Amarillo De La Aurora
Boreal como Las
Vinos Anoche:

we ride
the AURORA
like 2
Notes in
time-Less
trance-jence

S.

S.

11 oct:
Mendenhall
glacier:

citrine, amber
& neon
rose madder

N.

Zenith

A shower of
Sp&itting, falling, ever-
recombining molecules
Sounding like JAVANESE
gamelon... lime green
milk in Alluvial fans
from the Alizarine
Breast of Night....
her Magnetic fingers
parting the
Divine Seam
so that Light
Pours upon us
From the other
Side...

N. De JOAQUIN
OR Giovanna... Lue do not
WG Know her who you are... the deaf sun
woman at the Bakery says you are more each Day:
but we Do Know we Love you
Oh First BORNE of OURS! - only 4 mos.
in your Womb House... if we hear you
making your
1st SOUNDS!

Poem from the Sanitary Fill

I saw America's textbooks from a flatbed today.
I pulled to a stop over the pit and pulled the handbrake.
I smelled a heap of nothing burning inside a crater.

I spied on things beautiful once standing as forests & mountains.
I laughed at the refuse America was built on.
I revved the engine and saw 347 seagulls lift their feathers & poop.

I opened the door, jumped out, walked over
empty heads of man, woman, families, children.
I picked up refried beans, air cleaners, water pipe, tennis shoes
adding machine tape, 7-Up & Chevron.

I jumped over bones, mittens, strawberries, Tide, nightgowns
sofas, old safes, broken rear ends, bowling pins, IBM
toy telescopes, Packard Bell & Weber's Bread.

I stood on everything what used to be, still is & always will be.
I let a wad of jissom fly to symbolize man's masturbated mind.
I heard a Boeing 707 & claimed it a UFO.

I ate a Baby Ruth, read Man's World, Young Romance & Archie.
I saw society in an orgasm, things on top of things, climaxing.
I overheard distant fire sirens, air raid, schoolbell.

I bent down on two knees, coughed, and wept for the sake of it all.
I proclaimed man would be an idiot before he is brave
    & make a fool of himself when he is finally free —

Alaska, 1968

America End of the Workers Season

america lunchtime rows
of men on lumber piles & boxes
arms at right angles, 45 minutes til whistle
blow, elbows on knees   hands hanging between legs
backs bent, white bread raised into mouths
banana peel in sawdust, Lucky Strike
match smothered by shoe, conversation
in pairs   small group here
another over there
a loner
two loners,   three

america eyes without movement
daze pre-fixed between thoughts into nowhere
another bite outta the sandwich
an open jaw, an open ear, a dead-silent chuckle
that starts somewhere down within
& never reaches top
a tear that does the same
a sneeze
a guffaw
a curse
a tubercular cough laid green
on wet cement
a word or two about the old man
about the wife
about no overtime last week, how Shorty
found a plastic fork inside his club sandwich
yesterday down at the Ice Breaker

america three months fair weather
coming to an end construction slow, fish season
dying, raining heavier
loggers stand still, roadwork froze
men laid off

america down the street left
into the Imperial Bar
crowbars left hanging, gloves emptied of hands
flags by roadsides, Cat empty, earthmover

idled down, Peterbilt up the road
wheels cocked duck season beginning
crack of weapons fall of birdprey

america thermos cap unscrewed
coffee steaming in wet southeaster air
canning machines stopped dead
chopping boards cleaned, walk in set at 45 below
aprons, rubber boots, hats hung
in nude-poster locker rooms
knives scrapers hats slimers buckets
put away, floors washed down
corner snack-stand closed
dock barbwired no tresspassing
no fishing

america first snowflake mixed with rain
home from school early crying rheumatic fever
wife pregnant doorstep falling apart
light rent heat due
kerosene stove on the blink motor dead toilet
frozen coffee stain won't come out
soused again tonight, chapped hands
cold neck, a stinging back-alley piss
a tabletop hangover, can smell it
in the kids room

america I'd leave you but
it wouldn't be good enough for you
Why don't you do something around here?
Fix the window find some cardboard
get some masking tape, jam the seams & holes
Shut up! They're my affairs
I'll handle em Don't come around here askin
You hear? Be quiet! Goddamn,
you're never home anyway
Well what for, when this is just as bad
a trap as out there? Why not!
When there's nothin here for me, no money
no job, everything spent
before ya get in the door, what the hell!
What can you buy when you *do* have it?

What the shit! You can go to hell!
What for? When I'm already there
Close that door make your own dinner
O God, the kid's cryin again
it's your fault, No,
it's *yours*! O no
O goddamn

O goddamn america!

Juneau, Alaska
X. 68

IV.

from
LOOKING FOR MINERALS
(1975)

for Gioia

"But this dark is deep;
now I warm you with my blood, listen
to this flesh.
It is far truer than poems."
— Marina Tsvetayeva

SUR OESTE 21.1.75

I am in the rocks today: under the clouds what was once surrounded by black + sun-glazed. molten, now black + sun-glazed. On one side Frozen in the Wind. On one side of me, a star-born man zooms down, etched waist-high in the rocks. To another side a fighter-jet pierces the air...

Not one Desert flower save for those pistils stamens & corollas marked on stone by the old ones: on this 1st Day of SPRING!

ANASAZI VERSION of LAO TZU?

...a star falls & disappears ...that is to say: it enters our Galaxy &: a new SOUL is born!!

the Old 'Ones did some Sorcery with the Horizon: ———— : they bent it into a O or a ⊙ they separated the O into ∩∪∩∪ and bent these rainbows or waterholes into ⌐⌐ : steps linking heaven & earth: gods and ⊙ mortals..: Or: | + — = + ⊕ the intersection of heaven + earth, man + woman, the 4 Seasons within endless TiME

22.3.75: to create MUSIC as we walk... & thus step into Eternity

the Body is A Map... folding & unfolding into myriad dimensions; Earth a primordial Etching in the MiND... Eve's garden a circle ⊙ in God's ✳ the Body is a STONE MIRROR Between land + Sky: Stick-Figure & anatomy ⊰⊰ animal-track Heart Beat...... the Body is a MAGIC WOMB on all Fours: a petroglyph of Brittle air + Blood vanishes with dark Streaks of OLD SUNLIGHT..

It is Spring Now

The stars rush out
with a special odor through the waving pines.
There are sparks in my mouth. A whirling universe
stands still on the blue beach of our bedcovers.
Nobody is dancing but us.

It is a great dance floor
& we are simply alone. It seems like
an eternity, then out of nowhere spectators applaud
from the walls. All is finished.The lights dim.
Your fingers slowly release
their grasp.

It is spring now,
aroma of sage & lucious portions
of ripe juice from little fruits peeled beneath your eyes.
Everything in bloom!
Beyond the windows, a severe wind picks up.
I watch the blossoms spin through
the deepness of night

And feel the greatness
of your smile, forever warming me.

Guadalupita
New Mexico, 1973

From the Seat of a Farmall Super A Tractor

Frontwheel in the purple furrow
lift & lower the hydraulic rudder, ah
blusterous cloud, pink rock canyon walls
I can't plow. Fresh black earth
turned into sun —

Eyes to the axle, oxide orange
along the thin driveshaft, a turquoise wire
to the wobbling headlight. Bounced from
the seat, cushioned into cumuli
spare parts rattle in the clamped box —
I wonder, would I make a good
farmer?

Sometimes, like in a mad poem
my fingers drift from the wheel, my head
flings off its body. Then the plowshare
barely skims the land, maybe only nips
the horse turds. Like always
I rebound back into the act, the clatter
of the machine, drop the blinding rudder
deeper than ever along the edge
of the field.

Smoke

Living, like smoke
       curling upward into rain
Smelling like smoke, twisting
       laying flat like smoke

Rings, around our heads
       around our fingers, wreaths
made of smoke

Smoke!
Smoke demons! Smoke
       eyes & mouths. Smoke wrapped
in our clothes at night

Smoke from campfire
       from lightning-singed trees.
Smoke from flint & steel
       & pineneedle tinder

Smoky water to wash in
Smoked soup, smoke
       an eggplant peel. Smoked
sticks of love

Like effigies in
       the rainstorm passing

We are the Smoke gods
       lost at mesa bottoms, in
canyons, chanting, drifting
           laying, curling
     falling
       long & flat

In the night
       Smoky arms, smoky legs
       Smoke in our lips, tongues
        of smoke

       In eachother.

Looking for Minerals

Opal, amethyst —
your moon-draped florid mound.
Whispering hair I thresh, gothic windows
you see through.

Mars, Neptune —
jade stream, opaque stone,
fingers that twist the nippled hill.
Seafoam rush & suck of blood,
phosphorescent pool you draw me into.

Jurassic, Cambrian, upward folds—
lavish meridian my hands wander over.
Salt, oil, uranium.
The world spins as we grow old,
gets faster & we die young.

Let's lay back
against these porous walls,
pick lodestone from breccia cliffs.
Watch serpentine glow under strontium flame,
form new spectrum through the scope.

Hydrosphere, Ionosphere —
sensuous valleys up & down your spine.
Mineral hunt, prospect.
Loops of platinum, cobalt glass;
native copper behind these clefts
I pick, these geologic doors
to Eternity.

A Night in Early Autumn
After a Clearing Storm

It is a small night
& I am caught not quite awake nor asleep.

Yes, tonight is infinite
& insignificant enough to undo
a thousand knots
    —an open cantaloupe on the table
    —a pitchfork dancing under the stars

You at the doorway, brushing your hair
    —the small dark curve of your breast
        against the wall
    —a little bit of anxious laughter
        in my jazzed skull

I can say nothing.
As you come to bed I turn the flame
   down low; only the still, moist air
to circulate our rumors.

Not much to say, I move over,
        almost afraid to touch you.

From afar, in night's tiny window
comes an ozonous burst of lightning
   to hold us inside its flash.

In this emptiness there is little form;
everything moves on its own
            —unforced

All these years with you
& only now, in the smallest part
of night
      do I begin to
        understand.

It Will Get to Be Ten Below

But we will be here.
No way out of this cold, but to keep moving.
And yet we end in the same place.
Wolf tracks circling wolf tracks, paw print
inside paw print.

You lose your mind, then slowly
your body. Fingers fall off.
You cannot walk.
Eyes bleed. Vision fogs.
Nothing left.

It will get to be ten below.
We will tire of running, & face up to it.
Rations are miles away.
All roads impossible.

The slicing wind
which has kept us from keeping still
for so long, will subside.
In the cold, we will come to know
each other again.

With a sense of opening, I won't
have to strain to enclose you.
Our kiss will free us from the snow.
The body will begin to
repair itself.

Places where there was nothing
will grow back.
The seasons
            — self healing.

Searching for Owls on a Snowy Eve

A dark evening in March.
In unison, two owls hoot from
the snowy pines.
I move closer, but they won't let
me come near.

Between their calls
I stop, listen to the snow
fall upon my coat sleeve
aware of the space in the lull
created by the absence
of their hoot.

It is the song of secluded
accompaniment, the cry
of these birds. I turn in the snow,
walk back to our cabin, lit
with only one light.

eye writes for awhile, mouth seas
for awhile, ♡ yearns for awhile, Hand
sun shines, fish swim, moon sleeps
& Day BRAKES for awhile, nights for awhile,
awhile,

V.

from
ANDEAN TOWN CIRCA 1980
(1978)

Calle 9 de Octubre: kids Between doorways skipping around with rubber snakes, candles Ray Balls, rhyme Songs & Rope....

"Dolores La Loca Tiene Una
Boca Llena de Caca
Para tu Boca Que te
Provoca..."

guayaquil
verano 77

Andean Town Circa 1980

People here drink instant coffee
wear orlon, talk of Sputnik
& Che under Italian tapestries of JFK.

Kids with twisted scapulars around
pimply throats tease the meringue lady in
her University of Idaho sweatshirt
five sizes too large

Compliments of C.A.R.E.

A friar kills time with his parrot
watching dice players from an oxbone doorway
while the accordian player sticks out
a cup, pulls a plastic bag over
his head in the rain.

At one end of town, the village creep
wipes his nose, peddling plaster jaguars
holding in his hernia, selling two
for the price of one.

At the other, under
the general's poster, a girl tends three goats
who look like men dressed as beasts
ready to eat his words.

Photographic Attempt, San Roque Market

I can't press the shutter anymore.
The scenery won't yield.
My lens folds in on itself, cursing in a voice
all its own. I can't walk through the fish
stalls, the banana mart or butchery.

Each time, my mind draws symbols that mix
with reality & I develop negatives
impossible to print.

I can't get close to the mortician
playing solitaire over a lacquered casket, along
the bloody aisle where the grocer's wife
puts her foot in my basket & winks
a missing eye.

I can't take any more shouts of
dying fathers & half-expectant nuns. Of alley
worts & wilted flowers. Or the elephant-foot
man in his wire cage, painting portraits
of the Virgin of the Swan.

Instead, I've tried my best to forget
knowing all the while that if I could, I'd
sweep everything back through the shutter
& remake the world, as it was
in the beginning, new.

Guayaquil / July 22

Alone on a jetty, nothing to do
my watch picked off on a bus, Calle 18th.
I beg a shoeshine from a kid
who reads Kaliman in his spare time.

Demagogs hide in stucco buildings;
orange peelers starve down below.
A Sister of Mercy walks off a destitute sloop,
an Indian strapped in the breakwater
with her cast-iron lugage.

A gypsy stands over a silver crucifix
splashed with miraculous water
writing oracles for humpbacks.
A secretary from Gloria Gorelik crosses
a gangplank littered with fish heads.
Dockworkers stare up her skirt, snuff
cigarette butts with bare heels.

I return to my father-in-law's
parting my hair like I always do when
I'm confused: three different ways.
On the promenade, behind two bronze boars,
the tide ebbs in. A lover feels up another
lover on a bench made of pink cement.

It's dark when I awake from my nap
& time to eat. There are conversations, but
I hear no one talking. Only a lamp above
the table keeps me centered.

Today, I have been too far
& frightened over what I've seen to make
sense of papaya served on crystal platters
while the news broadcasts another great
speech by another great leader
in another great country, north of the equator
on trans-oceanic tv.

Conch Diggers on the Esmeraldas Coast

Pole the canoes off
into mangroves, dig into the mud
come up with bloody hands
"While our men work upstream, $2 a day
come back after dark, torn clothes
legs cut by vines."

When that old skunk of a cargo boat
arrives, women & kids get 80¢ for each
hundred conch. With luck, the whole family
might have collected 300 conch.

That's $2.40 a day for a hell of a load of work.
Middleman takes it all. He gets $12 in Guayaquil
for that 300 shell.

"Be nice for us conch diggers to have
our own boat, sell direct — make the profit
ourselves. But not even all of us
put together have enough money to get started.

"Banks weren't made for conch diggers,
the politics don't allow for it."

Examination of the Old

At first they ask them, How did you get to be
one hundred & twenty-seven?

The old ones don't know. They aren't even
sure they *are* that old. But the doctors investigate
the civil registrar's birth books

And what did you eat?

Coffee when there was coffee meat when there
was meat rice when rice & when there wasn't anything
why, we didn't eat anything at all.

What was it like in the old days?

Well, used to be one *real* would buy you sixteen
eggs, but there weren't any *reales.*
Now everybody's got the *reales.* But there
aren't any eggs.

They are not satisfied, these scientists
with all the answers they get to their questions.
So they begin attaching wires & taking data.

You *are* a hundred twenty seven, aren't you?
We have proof that you are . . .

Until they pretty much convince the old ones
that they are too old to be alive!
And suddenly they die!
Die off, just like that —

Now the professional people move into
the village, making it over for tourists
with a new hotel called HOTEL SACRED VALLEY OF LONGEVITY

And this brings us right into
exactly what they wanted
                    — the twentieth century.

Time Exposure, Downriver

Six of us in a dugout canoe.
The bishop with canvas hat & privileged shoes.
Scarlet ribbons & sacraments.

The mathematician's logical smile & sore eyes.
A little scared, his books & clipboard
wrapped from paddle-splash in polyurethene.

The village nurse, aware, committed.
Her chapped hands quietlly clasped. A metal box
full of medicine at her feet.

In front & back are two from Taisha's tribe.

Naked, with their oars, they avoid whirlpools &
cut through undertow to land us.

Saying nothing, they drop us & pole back upstream
while we juggle our belongings, wondering
about our purpose.

Together, trying to find the path
we talk all at once, smelling of stale perspiration
in the tangled vines of moonlight.

Pangui
Upper Amazon

A Cathedral in Quito

Women chant Regina Caeli
as Eve deals an apple to a coiled snake.
Adam looks on, astonished.
A smiling Franciscan lowers the great white
Eucharist, while a no-neck sacristan
brings in calla lillies.

My palms turn backwards in their pockets.
Flames engulf sinners under an erotic
virgin whose topaz eyes triumph
on a black crescent moon.

In front of the church
a woman with scars on both wrists
sells crucifixes from a rusty Quaker Oats tin.
Next to her is an infant in cardboard box.

In this cathedral, I want to sin!
I want to lift the skirts of that virgin
who always & immaculately triumphs.
I want to take her into one perfectly dark
confessional for several hours.

I want to act foolish
& penetrate the cause, release this religion
from its chaotic cyclone of devils & cherubs.
I'd prefer goats to run loose with
gods, priests to turn into worshipers.

I'd like to have the hands
of that woman, alive & merciful — outside
on the steps of this church
solidly replaced
          in the world.

Sacha Runa Fiesta

Amber faces in the fog.
High at the world's top, men reclaiming
themselves as beasts:
        pumas monkey apes tapir clowns
& feisty diablos.

Pigs & anteaters flank a woman
dressed in yellow aprons, the hand of a mammal
painted between her legs.
A ghost-of-the-past hairy brown bear
enters Mariano's patio, humps up & down
        making love ferociously to the earth.

Reed flutes & rockets.
Knob-headed justers with deformed mouths
& broken megaphones impersonate
high government officials, & chief-of-state.

Then, the Danzantes.

Elaborate children of the sun, costumes of
carnelian & blue satin, whistling through narrow
hallways into cinder-ash landscape
        — brass bells, embroidered deer hooves
glass dolls & fake pearls glued to headboards
        dangling with bull horns & mirrors.

Hot red beasts in pen-&-ink rain
who chase wigged politicians in ridiculous
ripped skirts, with toy cameras
& plastic stethoscopes around their necks.
        Bear beasts   Danzante men!
Children with cowbones
        beating wooden drums.

At the end, drunk on chicha
my blank eyes fix far into myself
        with the madness of it all!
While hundreds of people assemble & dance
into a deep green crater,

I descend toward the plaza
& shake my horns like
the Danzantes — into the mirrored
glitter of my own
Soul.

Salasaca, Ecuador
VIII.77

STAR NUBE + SOL TREE SUN LOVE MOON eye

fog on SINCHOAgua,
Pasochoa wreathed
in snow...
Pomegranates &
Stringbeans in
white Enamel dishes
under black awnings
Burning trash &
HAIR clippings
blowing from run-
Down Barbershops
in the approaching
Storm

ah, Día de
mi SANTO
& I am at home
where I carry it: the
dot on the map
Fills my own 2 shoes,
goes where I go...
Stops where I stop.

the DANZANTES! all
part of a pre-Incan
RITE WHICH SURVIVED
both INCAN Socialism &
Spanish Feudalismo~
glitter of Breastplates
& HEADboards: pinned
& sewn with plastic dolls
money, crosses, glass
Jewels, film CANNisters
pearls & Tinfoil.

Mariano tells me
when Europeans came
& took the gold, they
were really stealing the
SUN... so the mtn. people
~Niños Del Sol~
replaced the gold with
coins; then the coins
with mirrors, & finally
...the mirrors with
tinfoil... Candy wrappers
& import pie plates.

WIRE GAROTA
SCREEN MASK
DANZANTE FACE
WIG HEAD COIN
SHIELD LINEN
PANIS HOMBRE

& the Cross is really + A STAR
shedding
Light
.to ignite
the ♡!

VI.

from
RITE FOR THE
BEAUTIF ICATION
OF ALL BEINGS
(1983)

Rite for the Beautification of All Beings

Give me a bundle of arrows
& a rainbow with a rectangular center, four dotted eyebrows
& a quiver of blue sky to contain my runaway thoughts.
Slip a cross of laurel under my pillowcase, blindfold an angel
with cellophane & run her three times around
the pomegranate tree.
I want an orange, a coffin, a pearl for my birthday.
Tell me I will die & quickly rise back to life with a future
sweetheart. Transcribe our names in a nuptial banana stalk,
save the sap to annoint my forehead.
Warn me against albino cockatoos, summon the prominent families,
the itinerant actors, the shepherds, wheelwrights,
medicine ladies & ranch hands.
It is dusk on the high desert, dawn in the galloping crevice.
Come along now, bring your sickles & gourds.

Let's disentangle the clenched fists & grounded ships.
Release the panting acrobats from the eyes of the chameleon.
Prepare the moats, stack the chips, turn the guards
around in their boots. Tempt them with unexpected acts of
tenderness in the face of sour-eyed dictators, whose
effigies we snarl & string up in the central square to burn.
Summon the illicit camels, the anemone & songbirds.
Save the cops & robbers for tv, while I heat up last night's
chianti & drink down the world in circles, licking away
imposters who move in straight lines.
Make room for smiling wheelbarrows of rice & shrimp.
Hail the children with phallic balloons.

Give me horehound candies, sudden crops
of early sunglow the day after my resurrection, thousands
of participants drinking fluorescent rum in a procession
of wild shouts, Nepalese yak bells & Hindoo drums.
Let there be a circle of onlookers
beating tortoise-shell gongs, blowing panpipes, freely
distributing Lotus-brand Burmese fireworks
& green spearmint tea to bring forth erotic desires.
Celebrate this during Passion Week, with ashes & palms
on the Thursday after Trinity Sunday
on the Eve of Saint John's.

This is what I'd like:

Let all songs be thoroughly inebriated.
Let guitars turn into tabernacles. Have Saint Peter
salute seagulls. Strip Adam & Eve of unnecessary fig leaves.
Arm yourselves with religious scapulars & wet fish heads
to prevent hysteria. Eagerly dismount the virgins
from their Calvary pedestals. Permit kangaroo rats & wire
haired terriers to line single file for a parade
through the Capitol. Untie the alligators
from the clocks. Make it mandatory that educators bow
before schoolchildren with armloads of geraniums.
Turn the intersections over to runaway mangos.
Give the crossing guards Clark Gable eyes & Bridget
Bardot mouths.

Is Henry Miller in the crowd?
Could he release the Sisters of Immaculate Conception,
that they might join with the Brothers of Mercy?
Cut off the answering service.
Provide a chalice that all may drink of uninhibited climax.
Hold these events in a basilica whose muscular nave
leads back to immortal jazz.
Hire Count Basie & Dizzy Gillespie, the Foursquare
Baptist Choir, & falsetto Tallahassee revival singers for
three days & sixteen nights. Baptize me a born-again believer
in ecstatic journeys through the over & under worlds
of dream & hallucination. Give me agnostic toothpaste
& trembling papyrus. Politicians dining with mermaids.
Manikins speaking in their native dialects.

Perhaps there's a genie in the multitude?
A soothsayer?
Is Jean Harlow present?
What about Charles Atlas, Sri Ganesha,
Walt Whitman?
Let's join in vivid triads & forget our marital status.
Let's crack jokes, play tricks, disorient the fox.
Let's keep all deep emotions impromptu.
May it last for nine months & twenty-two moons
with endless pulque & rayon skirts, cats & dogs dressed
in serpentine ribbons. Fireflies doing the honors,

farmers decked in fishscales. Keep it simple,
graceful. Propelled by primary colors, barefoot & infamous
with overlapping needs & miraculous intercession.

Keep no written records. Let June fall in November, as I whirl
happily with a charming señorita who jumps all over me
in her heliotrope wardrobe, obedient to solitude, bending her
back sideways, inhaling luxuriant smoke, rubbing purple
dust & so-called "Lucky Hand" brand sesame oil over her low-cut
Frederick's mail-order bra. And I will become eyeless &
submissive as we pierce all time barriers & hidden recesses
of the heart, on a small wooden platform covered with
creeping vines & frightening paper gargoyles.

Hire iguanas to open exquisite passageways
through wings & bellies of condors, through mute
underground laccoliths. Have a castle there waiting, tiled
with lodestone, burnished with King-Tut decorations
& a message from Amelia Earhart inside a little
box without instructions, covered with plastic roses &
ivory hearts, that plays Cole Porter when opened
— that pops out an upsidedown Chagall donkey in flight over
the Volga. Dim the balconies. Untax Johnnie Walker.
Allow Cannabis to remain wild.
Legalize green olives. Set aside several nights of
intimate friendship to commemorate the dead.
Gather with essence of bayberry, abracadabra singsong
of crickets & carnivorous tickling of uncaged feathers.

Put away the petroleum jelly, the nuclear fuel,
the Peabody steamshovel & twenty-four changes of
business week suits. Ban military takeover, sweep away
cynical choirmasters, untooth the fairies of disaster.
Cover your thighs with crushed marigolds, put back
your teeth & melt down the earwax. Burn the earwax
instead of Arabian oil!
Have gratitude, fear of the dark. Have no violent
arguments with Christ childs or hermits.
Engage in comic relief while jumproping the tails
of devils. Recall original significance
of barbaric dances, whirlwinds, breath-taking
waterfalls. Keep the identity openly

secret. And on the last day, pack each other's
belongings. Declare no winner.

Hang your umbrellas in the elevator.
Call back the airplanes from the moon. Recompose
your childhood from open groves of abandoned
alphabets. Have more than spiritual commitment.
Genuflect before windmills. Choose an enthusiastic
volcano. Leave a silent kiss on its neckline.
Paint my forehead with raw umber while you chant in F minor.
String together the Cross & Dipper as you
collect yourselves in ridiculous pink masks
& Bombay import double-breasted suits, while I recline
with my bride, my bandit sweetheart.
Take hold of the Bishop's robes, saddle my pony.
Tell the violinists we are ready!

Take time now, to remember.
Burn the thought of ever returning.
Be like the prayermakers who have special power
over the weather. Carry votive lamps into the grainfields.
Plant again innocence. Coronate ecstasy. Keep
knowledge tame. Be inconspicuous with virtue, be patient,
unarmed, always ready, totally unprepared.
See clearly what is to be done. Hold down disappointment
as you return to your native land. Arrive without
tether or foothold. Stand me upright on a dilapidated path,
send me on my way with a straw hat & a bear at my side
dressed in twinkling mirrors. Save the flash bulbs
& polaroids for my unequaled lover, my son, my daughter,
my wife, the lover of my wife & his lover, the other
lover of my lover, & all lovers yet to be born from
reunited lovers up there above this feasting
in the harpsichord stars.
Acknowledge madmen & frivolous liturgy
arm in arm. Have no explanations other than
courtesy. Remember courage, hope, the silent pivot of
sleep, the borders of dream.
Remember the multitude, the appropriate & reoccurring
clarity that supercedes wisdom. Have in mind
Sunday drivers, quick & unpredictable turnabouts,
cow crossings & cul de sacs. Hold close

to the flower, the staff. Do not allow your accepting
& rejecting to keep you from perfect balance.
Know your landing gear when the myth explodes.
Turn books rightside in, prune their pages at midnight.
Nothing endures. The word can't get by on reason alone.
Chaos controls order, infinity is shaped like a horseshoe.

Carefully take back what you said about illusion.
Do not be so busy that you cannot wander freely.
Get down on all fours to see out of your mind.
Be inactive with want, genuine with desire,
aware of excess, alive & explicit with ever-enduring thanks.
Go ahead with what you thought to be infinitely out
of grasp.

All have entered the singular eye of delusion.
All have been swept clean of ultimate realizations.
All have had enough of perfection.
All have been uselessly tied to thinking.
All have at one time or another blamed the innocent.
All have inconsciously taken steps into emptiness
from which a part of them has never returned.

I have strength to say it.
I have my lover within me.
I speak from the deep down heart.
I speak from the relative eye of fact.
I speak with blood & motion beyond language.

I go now, I will be . . .
She goes now, she will be . . .
He goes now, he will be . . .
You go now, you will be . . .
All goes now, all will be . . .

: all have entered
the singular Eye/i
of Delusion

: all have been uselessly
tied to thinking

: all have subconsciously
taken steps into
emptiness

from which no part
of them has ever Returned Ṗ..

VII.

from
POEMS AT THE EDGE OF DAY
(1984)

for Radha

"*Even the man who is happy
is touched with a longing he does not recognize.
It must be he is remembering a place out of reach, shapes
he has loved in a life before this, the print of them
still there inside him, waiting.*"

— Kalidasa

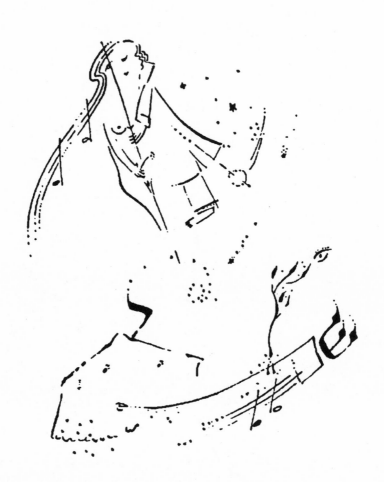

Poems at the Edge of Day

I want to see
how the puzzle fits, each word
every participle
the cog in the wheel
the blood in the stone.

Poems are acts of death
burning clean
at the edge of day
to renew life.

I want to step
into the house on the promontory
knowing well the cliff
that holds it
is held in turn by the Hand.

I want to see
how the puzzle fits, and you
are invited
into the house, the poem
the blood, the wheel
the stone.

We Speak to What is Blossoming
What Listens is Shedding Its Leaves

The orchards cast
spider shadows across the soil
and farmers in the river valley
burn out the ditches today.

Now water travels clear
with mirrored stones and sparkling eyes
through the ashes.
Spring is blessed
with blooming shadows,
the old voice burnt clean
of weeds and thicket

The dual rays of memory
and what is to come
transfigured into a single diamond,
a branch of song
and rivulets of questions
which don't ask
            to be answered.

Srinagar, Kashmir

Song for Eve

You were born
from the Maker's rib, not mine.
You were asked
into existence
by the serpent of water
who circles the sun.
You were made human
not to be my opposite
but for another step
in the dance.

Woman
whose kernel holds
Eternity,
eat the fruit of Eden, make
my world as you
touch it.
through me love the One
I love through you.

That Which Offers Itself
Hold It Like the World Up to Your Face
Take It Seriously — Rilke

The enigmatic loss
of speech as the body's raft spins
need not be explained.
The night is autonomous, the soul
is a voice in a tree
and it is as is
is: a pine
    a luminious pine.

By itself, breathlessness
is pure and sudden
as is coming upon a tidepool
with its alliance of plankton, stars
and mollusk   — serene
with their statements
as we mortals, in ephemeral repetition
of renewals, should be serene
with dawn
               — vast dawn.

For a Girl on the Beach of Seven Towers

We are shadows
wedded to a different sand.

"I liking you
           you liking me"

I've a soft spot
holding a thousand petals
of fear.

In the jungles
of Mahabalipuram, stone snakes
make a bouquet of their bodies.
But I am not so sure
of us. The starfish you give me,
blue jasmine I place
around your neck.

This morning
you want me forever.
By noon your tears will fill
the temple garden.

Mahabalipuram
South India, 1979

It is a Long Time Since I Have Asked Heaven
for Anything and Still My Arms Have Not Come Down

— Antonio Porchia

You are not sure
are you? I am not sure am I?
Thus flagged
how can the mountan be climbed?

A cairn steps aside
as we hit the pass. A thousand hollows
sing with white teeth in noon heat.

The sound carries up to us
under a child's paper kite. You take me
in your arms wearing a crown
of chiseled ice.

Like a woodblock impression
on handmade paper, my seed soaks
through your page with fibers
of black light.

Our flesh is the word,
two questions that disappear
in the song
of a thousand hollows.

Machhapuchhare, Nepal

Homage to Fire Which Quenches All Thirst

Inside woman is a seashell
and in the seashell is an ark

Inside the ark is a village
and in the village the world

Inside the world is a star
and in the star a flower

Inside the flower is Adam's seed
and in Adam's seed a key

Inside the key is a candle
and in the candle a map

This map was pressed to my lips
many lifetimes ago

I was a stranger
inside igneous stone

And You were fire
quenching my thirst.

To You O Goddess O Light Through Whom All Things Moving and Motionless Shine

When I knew you in innocence
I found what I was seeking.

When I became lost inside you
I no longer remembered what it was
I had found.

When the colt I tamed
backed out of its fields
with flared nostrils smoking,

When the doe cramped into agony
between the whirlpool's liquid teeth
and my books burned in your eclipse

I again remembered the essence
of the stream
I had been following.

I put my feet
into the soul of purity, and found
inside the wheel of a caravan

An angel speaking quietly
in the embrace of your dance
in the phoenix of your song.

For Radha, Nightfall

A red dress
A forget me not, a hide and seek
with desire

A kiss on the ankle
A sparrow in a tower
of scribbled fire

A moon inside the hammer
A lark on the map of the surveyor
A spider behind my eye

A sandstorm for Allah
A veil between the rungs of the ladder
A beehive for the magician

A wishbone for the maiden
A dragonfly in the footprint
of the lizard

A dove from the treetrunk
A high mass
in your chariot

A red dress
A forget me not, a song
in the breath of your shadow.

Monkeys Know

Monkeys have got it on us.
They know it all, they began before God
in the Tree of Time.
They've been to heaven and back, they want no part
of the stars or bananas or billfolds.
They'd rather hang upside down, scratch themselves and spy,
revitalize internal organs, live on bread and leaves.

Monkeys begin before dawn.
Whole families fan out from alcoves, brush teeth
at river banks, sit in temples with erections,
breast feed and speculate.

Monkeys manicure their toes,
wink at the sun, steal city clockdials
and balance their account with the second hand.
They swivel away with disgust at human war
and don't wear belts or drive cars.

Monkeys give thanks for silver fur.
They've played this human game before.
They've decided to advance the score.
They keep an open account with Adam, balance their checks
with the swing of a tail, say goodnight to the moon
and keep just a little ahead of evolution.

Monkeys have got it on us.
They carry no letters of recommendation
and file no affidavits. They walk to the center of the ring
with keen dark eyes, and pitch pennies backwards to man
who waits wearing shoes and neckties.
They've seen this show before.

Monkeys know.

— Swayambhunath, Nepal

OUR GEOGRAPHY IS HEARTBEAT

We all hold
to some territory.
The merchant makes his salad
with money.
The seamstress begins
at the fine-line stitch of time.
The astronaut remembers the Red Sea
with the ultra-violet eye
of the bee.
The dictator cuts apart geography
on his human meatboard.
The poet begins inside his mother
and ignites villages and trees
along the edge of the sea.

We all begin
as mirrors, naked
with bodies once solar
begetting form.
The priest wears a robe.
The judge wears a robe.
The scholar graduates in a robe.
All remember the alphabet differently.
All connect the swan with a proverb
or a symbol, or regard the stars
with possibilities.
And look to the craftsman
for a sewing bobbin
or a shoelace.

We all hold
to some territory.
The saddhu pins a marigold
between the breasts of Kali.
The evangelist eats out
on donations sent to convert pagans.
The orphan rides a subway
into black paradise, free.
The dragonfly holds 10,000 worlds
in its topaz blink.

And the fortune-teller looks through amber
to discover the handprint
of an assassin.

We all sit down
and rise inside a dream, asking
questions about our situation,
perplexed with lowering semaphores
that announce no train.
Some of us have stood up
on a rollercoaster,
opened a briefcase in
an airplane, or closed
a confessional door.
Some of us have arranged our hair
in an automobile, or put our legs around
a camel, on a trail into
the Empty Quarter.

Our geography is heartbeat
and a second hand swings
through the flesh, like a road
pretending no end
while outside the self
lives another One of us, who conducts
the word with a spiral wand
and carries into us charts and maps,
earth and particles of air
that combine to breed
water, fire, hate, love
passing storms
and gates that can be locked
or unlocked forever
among us all.

VIII.

from
THAT BACK ROAD IN:
SELECTED POEMS 1972-83
(1985)

"To go forward is to travel far.
To travel far is to return.
The Great Square has no corners.
There where there is nothing
the house is useful."
— Tao Teh Ching

The landscape is made portable as its Spirit
enters the FLESH, becomes Humanized, finds
dwelling, sings OUT again thru the Mouth

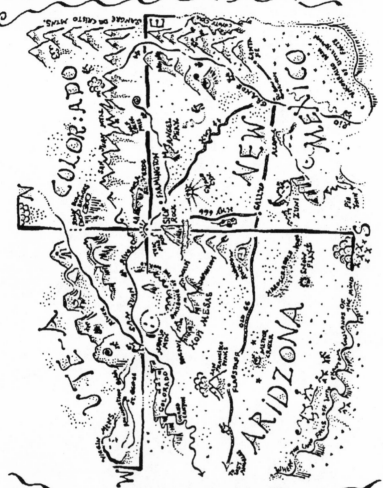

the Map begins within; geography ERUPTS
from the Imagination, becomes real as we
walk... disappears as we turn our Heads...
stays in the ☺ & in the MinD to SpeLL out
metaphors for a world BeyonD the one Before US

If They Ask

Tell them I'm gone for a week
up to Three Turkey Ruin
past where the pavement ends
along Yellow Jacket Creek

Tell them I'm sitting in the shade
on the road toward Ismay
eating white strawberries, under
a Four Corner moon

And that I took no naps
        — nothing to find my way.

Let them wonder
because I'm gone, receiving
news from nowhere
asking questions in the hills
        talking to lizards
            with my cap on backwards.

I urge you: Don't follow
                Don't ask why

I might be in a bar
at Mexican Hat, or retracing
my footprints in another dry gulch

Keep this journey quiet:
        like the wing of a dove
            against tan-gray stone

Like that time we made love
by Sleeping Ute Mountain
        scooping sandpits for our bodies
            along the banks
                of the San Juan.

These Places, Following Over

Bacavi, Shipaulovi
Kin-li-Chee
      Wide Ruins
      Window Rock

Passed through these places
& knew the taste of chili stew
      & mutton & wild pheasant
      smoked over mesquite.
Then on:
  Peach Springs
  Two Guns, Meteor Crater
      Jackrabbit —

Knowing every place
is but physical geography
  corresponding with the
      Heart Path.

Nazlini
Fluted Rock
      Acoma
— it *must* be enchanted.
That's where Simon
asked his father   "What's that place
      in the rock for?"

"Oh, *that* place.
  It's just where you feed
      the Wind."

At Mesa Verde

Ute-Liner, Travel-Craft
Weekender, Pace Arrow
   — man fromWalla Walla, wife
       from Savannah, kids born
in Arlington, face backwards
      3000 miles
    playing war in a Coup de Ville
         to get here.

Rangers give directions
to the snack-bar, not in metric
     but: "Go ten Winnebagos down."

Matadors, Gran Torino
Starcraft & Sportsman all empty
   americans pulling up
     to the Sun Temple

Up a 30 foot ladder
a thousand feet above the Mancos Valley
the woman I'm with wears no underwear;
   vacationing executive turns
      to his camera-eyed wife:
        "Got it on infinitive?"
Balcony House
tour proceeds — scout leader
  behind me secretly whispers:

"Gotta time this vacation just right.
  Wouldn't know what to do
    with any extra days
      starin' me in the face"

(his foot
  in a pre-Columbian toehold)

& the dark-eyed woman
from Boulder, dressed in forestry-department
green, gives me the rap
   on Anasazi menstrual pads

under a red
handprint   in Longhouse ruins —

That same night
after the tourists left, we climbed
into an old kiva, smoked hemp
    found corncobs & hanks
        of gray yucca

Watched a white rainbow
    over Montezuma Valley, stoned
I carried myself away
        "Ten Winnebagos down"
            & 13 centuries back

        To how it was "then"
            When America was still
            without
                Name

The Woman Who Danced Into Heaven

It's a simple enough story.
It came back to me
when I was reading a poem by Luci
about how good her daddy used to sing
on the way back to Shiprock.

"He had a strong voice
       he would start singing in Navajo"

And that reminded me
of a Pomo Indian woman who would sing
in her bed in a nursing home
in northern California.
She'd be moving around, all over the place
throwing her covers off, chanting
& practicing dancing
       —that's what she was doing.

"I was sent back.
 I wasn't a very good dancer
 so I didn't make it into heaven.
      Now I'm practicing —every day
because pretty soon I'm going
to die again, & this time
      I want to dance real good.

"I want to know all the steps.
 You have to move just right
   if you want to get into heaven.
That's why I'm practicing dancing.
      So I won't have to come back again."

Some Reasons for the Gods

(Zuni Shalako, 1976)

This afternoon before the ceremonies
a few of us hiked to a sandstone cave, high in
a cliff face off the shortcut road to Gallup.
I hoped for some pottery shards
    but we found only recent graffiti:
          "CHARLES MADE LOVE TO ME"

Later, I realized that graffiti
sanctified a place where two people joined.
In the cave's pink glow, I felt the sun's warmth
impregnating the darkness   & thought the Old Ones
might have honored that same act
    by inscribing a quiet, unfolding spiral.

Afterwards, in Zuni, I walked
through the old part of town, sun lowering
behind huge stacks of gnarled juniper —just watching people,
smelling smells, feeling good about this village
that had nurtured me for so many years.

When the Kachinas clacked & jingled
down Greasy Hill, I followed them   shrine to shrine,
    these immortals mixing with mortals,
planting prayer feathers, inseminating our Mother
on whose breast the people dance
to keep the seasons turning in harmony.

From midnight on, the men
were busy with ritual, weaving creation stories
while the women (knowing well the process
of labor & emergence) went about
preparing bread, cooking mutton stew
    for the dancers

Everybody just a passing shadow,
Orion cresting high,   sparks mixing with stars
from outdoor ovens   womb-shaped mud ovens
from which shawled ladies removed perfect

baby-shaped loaves, & carried them into ceremonial houses
    to be blessed, broken   & shared.

In my mind, I returned
a half million years to when fire
was first enclosed by humans, circled with stone,
kept in one spot. In my body I was the dark phantom of Crow
    flapping house to house landing before painted altars
set with feathered wands, turquoise & crystal.
In each house, deer & antelope peered from the walls
through blankets & shawls, looking on from a mythical forest
of bright colors veiling their world from ours.

And I asked myself
    "Why is it these gods come?"

In my heart I knew the Kachinas were there
to remind us of a World Before, where we spoke
with the gods & danced as equals.
But now our dance is with mortals, & no matter how hard it is
to remember that dance done before, we must try.
To forget would be to remain on earth forever.
To remember the steps is to move through life with grace,
intuition, courage.   And to enter again
    the doors of Immortality.

It is this way at Zuni.
You step into the wings of a crow
You fly through light years of stars
You remember that to meet   is to begin to part.
To plant prayer feathers is to keep alive
      the thought of heaven on earth.
And to make love high on a cliff face in a cave
    is to bring back
        the beginning of time.

Angel Peak Overlook: A Road Song

John —

Get good & sick.
Sick of your self, sick of your body.
Sick at the sight of Peyote.
Vomit masks, attachment, distractons.
Have visions, confront ghouls.
Look hard enough at the demons & watch them
turn into sheep.

Sleep alone in a place you've always been afraid to.
Realize mortality, laugh out loud.
Be reduced to an ear, a shadow speaking through itself.
Wake with a song, clear your throat, become a child.
Enjoy the deep questions, even if they
have no answers.

Know the requirements of wisdom:

— to dance at least once in your life
      that the doors of heaven may open
— to make a fool of yourself completely
— to love, to be eaten, to die
— to become celibate & wander owning nothing,
                  always open to the road
— to find yourself in solitude
— to renew lovemaking, opening your eyes at climax
            to all those alphabets you never understood
— to get good & angry
— to grow older with humor & tenderness
— to use the fire lit by enemies on all sides of you to see by
— to let go of what you want & watch it appear
      at the door without asking

John —

    Don't fight what keeps you awake;
    rise exhausted & clean.
        Give it back, everywhere
            in the world.

Gods Eyes for Sale

(Sign near Red Lake, Arizona)

"You see the San Francisco Peaks way off there?
It's home of the kachinas. but if you drive
closer it all disappears. It's not the same place
you saw from back where you started.

"If you come to this country
you must learn to live with eyes that are not your own."

One time after the Hopi Bean Dance on Second Mesa
I drove away with a friend, 3 in the morning
still hearing deep ogre groans, falsetto cries
of monster mothers, whipper kachinas & owls.
Also began to see sharp beaks in the stars & bulging eyes;
& remembered being caught at Old Oraibi by a clown
who rubbed my face with soot.
I held grandfather David's hand after that
All the Hopis laughed & he said

        "that is *all* right"

Before dawn my friend & I
pulled into Keams Canyon, electric lights in the campground
& I thought   "a good safe place"
but she wanted to park way out where there was nobody
so I stopped in pure darkness on a mesa top.
She got out but ran quickly back in & locked the door.

        "Something's walking toward the car"

Before she could finish
a man's bulky figure was at the window. It bent down.
It had the face of a beautiful girl.
She said she'd been walking a long time, trying to
get back home. But the voice didn't come from her mouth
It came from all around her

"Maybe you can catch a ride down at Keams
from the tribal police," we said.

Without a sound, the figure vanished.
For the rest of the morning, I didn't sleep.
I had cold feet, & I kept hearing rachety moans, sawing teeth.
When the sun came up I walked around outside the car
but found no footprints in the snow.

"See, this is a different kind of wilderness.
Not like they show in books.
What makes it wild is that it's inhabited.
If the songs & planting & monsters & maidens
weren't here — it'd just be another place
to get away from it all."

You're given a different set of eyes here.
That's no metaphor.
Whatever you see with those eyes
isn't a dream of a vision.
    Because whatever you see you can reach right out
        with your fingers & touch.

                — that's what makes
                        it wild.

From Desert Journals / 1975

Macro. Micro.
Questions pose themselves in mirages,
batter the mind with delusions.
Contemplation. De-codification.

Pass over. Poke through.
What we write is not necessarily who we are
but more often a clarification of what we'd like to be.
Charting the depths. Narrowing the course.

Exploding myth. Aligning head, wheels, heart.
Gullies turned inside out. Earth the pivot point
where I dig in toes, grow food.
Move out from, return to.

Journey to balance great with small,
to know the deep, scale the impossible wall.
Journey to guard against becoming too easily arrogant
about 'my' place and closed to any other way.

Travel, plant knowledge.
Glean wheat, share economies, save pennyroyal.
Bring in the bumper crops, carve maps into rocks.
Quarry the rocks for hearth stones.

Later carry the stones
to a foundation site   & build a home.

map of Present (1.13.76) Mind State:
ever-journey-ing in thee ephemeral
wheel of TIME on with ☼'s ☾'s & ♥'s
primed to-ward ∿ THEE

GREAT HORIZONS OF LIGHT (NATION'L

(UNWMD)

SILENT & UNCHALLENGED PRISTINE BLUE OF GUT INTELLECT

CONSTANT AWE-ZONE INTER SHOW E?RS.

INSPIRING OF UN-RUPTED METEOR

WELL-SPRING & ever-burning arena OF BOUNDARY-LESS MINDS HEARTS

UN-TAMED FLOWER OF DIVINITY

CLEAR LITE TERRITORY OF UN-ENDING PEAKS

UNWEEDED PATH OF UNFINISHED HANDSHAKES

TO UNKNOWN REGIONS

The Great & Careful entrance

INSIDE VIEW OF THEE EVER UN-
WHOLLY & FOR-
FINISHED PLAN
OF
CREATION!

(A STAR-GAZER'S GUIDE TO THE MAKING OF CHILDREN

ESCAPING EVER MUSE

copico right from thee mind - by JOHN BRAND - 1976

PORTRAIT OF DOG WALKING ON ALL 4'S ...RESTLESS CIRCLES IN RESTLESS CIRCLES

UN-NEGOTIABLE VOID

TELE-PATHIC ANTENNAE

THIN-LINE EXSTATIC PATHS CHASING THEE UN-INHIBITED EVER

NOTICE HOW THEE DOG SPEAKS IN...

No Mattter What Road I Travel,
I'm on My Way Home —Shinsho

Windswept, out
of reach, spiraling in
        mind clear, at last
this evening with you.

It's not the pavement
that brings me back, but
a homing device:
        Hokusai curve of mesa wave
        Hawk over farmhouse
            in double-shaft of rain.

You know
the miles I've traveled,
    cities & field that burn
between my dark branches.

Will you take
this flower I carry?
This moon that sets fire
to all earthly ties?

Will you bend
a little closer — beyond the grasp
of mind, out of death's reach
        in this unfocused room?

Stand inside
the Painted Gate, wipe clean
the mirror — here inside you
        I'm found

Here inside there is no poem
to describe the feeling
for what it is that'll
        forever
            draw me
                back.

Homegoing, After Joaquin's Birth

There's nothing more to know
than what I am
when I touch the other side
of what I'd like to be.

Everything I've waited for
        Birth / Death
              is right inside this
                  den of mine

Mantra the trail
music a stream, into a circle
without doors
this headrest where I dream.

Ladyfern!
        fireflower   puffball
        paintbrush   jimsonweed

remember me
when I am gone, &
        you still sing.

Turning Thirty Poem

I am turning thirty
today half cloudy wheels spinning home alone splitting
wood plucking nopales wife out shopping for
crunchy granola kids down the creek splashing
dough rising in the porcelain sink
I am turning thirty

Suddenly Sunday by myself standing in front of
the mirror trying to decide on a guru
I am turning thirty

And don't have a guru!
no running water flush toilet garbage disposal
& I'm no good at astral projection
can't sleep on a spiked bed, get pimples
once in awhile & the roof always needs fixing
I am turning thirty

And can't roll a joint
still don't know when to take the bread out
rather have flapjacks & bacon with vermont maple syrup
or crepes suzette soused in lemon walnut yogurt & honey
with sausage & buttermilk instead of
"health food" any ole day
& don't like to fast except when I'm hitchhiking
I am turning thirty

And can't fix my car
still can't draw hands or feet
& my best friends call me the walking bust
because I got conjunctivitis
better known as "pink eye"
I am turning thirty

No life insurance
no stocks bonds heavyweight titles
varsity letters or books published by Dell
I am not a famous writer
I am not a famous painter

& my wife tells me
I am only "famous" in my own home
I am turning thirty

The cupboards don't shut right
because I made 'em the nopales don't
taste right
because I cooked 'em
the kids have reached puberty at the ages of 3 & 4
they're putting me down because I get angry restless
impatient & am "highly spiritual" only at the right times
I am turning thirty

trying harder every day
to match what I think I am up to the "real" me
I am turning thirty
thirty is turning me, I am up to my neck
in the cosmic wheel
in the clearing clouds, sunlight
thirty years old
wife bumping up the dusty road
11 o'clock muffler dragging, late summer night
constellations zooming through my head, kids in bed
cookstove cleared, cats purring
invisible wishful thinkings of wine spilled
over my leg from a warm glass of Dr. Pepper
turning thirty

Buddha rises in his shrine
our bare feet tiptoe up into the loft
sky breaks thunder, dog farts
a line storm breathes strokes of light
kerosene lamp quivers
my birthday is here, clothes off rain stopped
moon out coyote howling pinetrees shaking water
through the window wind blows cat meows
baby wakes fill the bottle, dawn light glimmers
early morning planets sway in celestial haze
have I gone *mad!*

I am not an astronaut
I am not the first man on the moon

as my friend Dr. Jomo would say
I have not broken any great records

I am thirty years old
& just plain fully awake
the earth is cosmic
& my woman is really her own lady
our bed is mulched with war surplus foam
cool sheets in between our legs
it is fall

Going into winter
going into spring going into summer
another time another place another year
& my birthday suddenly doesn't mean a thing

I am thirty years old
tonight, watching the wheel go round
& building my hearth out of
pyramids of light.

Poem, First Day of Summer

A pinecone pyre
set to light
by the children, coiled smoke
   on a green day in June
— the lay of the canyon
    & believable patches
        of sky

Each stone
   with imprint of hand & foot
gaining hold   every ridge
has me spellbound
    — nearer, perhaps

To you
than I could ever be
   in our togetherness, ah
this heart beats steady
   through latticework
of change   — & sets me
on course, once more
   without you   but within you
               always

      this
        green day of June.

Thank You Joaquin, 7th Birthday

Thankyou for your balsawood hummingbird,
for the white primrose you said smelled like
lemon romaine pie. For snoring in my ear
after reading Mouse Soup, & the jackrabbit
on the way to school.

Thankyou for wearing green pajamas
in daylight, flying your 30 foot long Chinese
octopus kite. For recognizing wild asparagus
& finishing my beer. For long nights of company
& short ones of fear.

Thankyou for wanting to go to college
to be a snake-charmer.
For your oatmeal-box factories, your packrat
tendencies, the Eveready battery collection,
the goose egg that fed us both for breakfast
& fireflies to read by.

Thankyou for being scared
of so many stars, for the worm in my apple
because he needs to eat, too.
For lightning storms turning trees into firewood
to heat us this winter. And the heart-shaped stone.
The beggars, madmen, & forget-me-nots.

Thankyou for copying page 22
of the *Rubaiyat of Omar Khayyam* & me not having
to tell you. For letting the White Sands box turtle go,
for the secret paths to cattail nests
left by redwinged blackbirds. For dreaming of day & night
at once, & not stepping on that antpile
you called a cliffdwelling.

Thankyou for no big words & all action,
for dressing as King Kong & making the rounds
with Electric Woman. For turning into Coyote
& shutting the radio down so I could hear him sing.
For noticing the man with no arms painting Popocateptl
in the park in Juarez on a Sunday morning.

For the 11 starlings dancing wire to wire
while I talked long distance to Truth or Consequences.

Thankyou for telling me that magpies keep
woodticks from giving people fever by catching them
off cows' backs. For saying to the nextdoor neighbor
who squashed a praying mantis: "It doesn't bite
& it's good for our garden."

Thankyou for being six, turning seven,
pretending to drive my truck when I am tired.
Knowing the planets when I am lost,
keeping courage because we are alive. Stealing
my Liquid Paper to paint a waterfall. Loaning me
your Star Wars flashlight to fix the fusebox
& investigate the deep-down depths of our broken
toiletbowl. Thankyou — because to thank
is to have hope.

Thankyou for telling me no,
for terms simply put — for the dark side of light.
For never running out of time, for believing
in volcanoes, & not saying anything when I exaggerated
the number of deer we saw at the bird refuge.
Thankyou for identifying the angels & naming no demons.
For the horseshoe anchor you tie to our porchpost
to keep dad from floating away during the day.

Thankyou because we are adrift on a crowded sea.
Thankyou, because we haven't forgotten how it seems.
Thankyou, for glaciers moving
slower than jets. And big leaves, silence
& riverbeds. Thankyou for sleeping
with the lights off. Thankyou
because you cry, too.

Thankyou because you've told me
others laugh at you. Thankyou for wanting me
alive. Thankyou again for that story of Coyote:
about that time he danced up out of the arroyo
hopping & wiggling his head, getting closer & closer
like that — then snatched one

of Mr. Gonzalez' chickens!

Thankyou, because I love you.
Thankyou, because the list could go on & on.

Thankyou, Joaquin.
Thankyou.

Prayer at the Bend of a River

for Regina Friske, 1906-1981

I light copal, Mother
& pray at the mountain's foot.
I sing *Regina Caeli*, recite old litanies
& mantras.

I wash three times,
circle myself with burning sweetgrass,
sing to the flashing water.
But I hear no prophet, I am listening
for you, Mother.

Blue willows bend in sunlight
as I cross my legs
& close my eyes, listen to the river,
talk to kingfisher
& swallow.

I hear you, Mother.
You are a raindrop in the current.
You are many women at once
speaking in thunderbolts.

You are a thousand raindrops
rising back to heaven
from the water in which I was born.

A Song for October

For reminders
of death & incarnation
I sometimes lay my blankets in twisted fashion
alone under Hesperus, pondering
    the Bear at our galaxy's end
& set myself straight
      in the tangle of changes
     making peace with terror & delight.

For reminders
    that death has no end
I lift my glass through broken clouds,
   cast my shirt into shadows of wild geese
& leave footprints
on a small path, watching sparrows
peck at my heels
      & fly off over horsemen
whose bells echo across idle lakes.

For reminders
   of the Great Ocean
that surrounds our universe
I paint thousands of fish in a crimson net
with a few floating through
                into deep blue.
For reminders
of you and me, I untie my heart
from any guarantee, lift my staff over
massive peaks, listening
   to animals bark
     through the dragging hours of night.

I call out your name
& catch myself smiling
     knowing in order to come close
    I have had to travel far.

Winter Poem

Late at night
    universe without quarrels or need:
no presidential elections
    — no president.
Nothing of newscasts, no murders
    or sabotage no ruling class
harnessing laborers
    or jailing hungry thieves.

Only crinkled shapes
    of earth; dogs barking   one   two   three;
old ones side by side, young lovers
    wrestling, while frost
crisscrosses fields & posts.
    Louder, louder
        — the universe hums.

I am carried far
into ancient flowers
into thick & cold waters;
    I am blown away, added to heaven
like a dead man is added
        to the stars.

Late at night
    I dwell in designs of rocks;
wake in the frost with a handful
    of immortals, I spy on myself
    still asleep with you
        & smile

    for it is early, & in the universe
    everything is new.

A Poem for the New Year

I am not writing poetry
these days but am talking in verse
to the ancients who prod me on & bless me
with stolen apples, or call to me
disguised as trees who sing to their shadows
in amethyst sand.

No need for poems.
I simply align my wheels
with Polaris, & coast in neutral uphill
writing letters to Persuasion, crossing
Thin Bear Creek
drinking long swallows of burgandy.

I visited recently
with the poet Issa, & he's doing well.
He has enough to drink on the withered moor.
He has his compassion, & things are boiling
in the saucepan.

No, I'm not writing poems
but making the rounds knocking at the gates
of waterbirds, following acrobats
into sunbeams, enjoying quick walks
into eternity, green shadows
of goats straddling night rainbows.

I've bowed my head
to peacocks in whitewashed shrines, heard lovers
in secret places making love
to other lovers' loves.

I like the moan
of tugboats & jeweled city rain
on plastic umbrellas, hot wet pavement
& glittering saltweed. I'm content to ride
the sharpened edge, & get by in the darkening evening
with a bowl of fresh nasturtiums.

No need for poetry

for I dance more these days
with fugitive crickets in unreluctant sunsets.
I'm doing more listening to the Body's changing attitudes
I've seen through it all here & there
— held roses to my head; heard the pulse
        of their breathing.

I've visited the pyres,
stopped scratching my bites.
The old passion has come back to me.
In every new face I focus on great beauty.
I sleep with rivers moving through my eyes,
& gently recognize each dream
            as part of reality.

I often marry invisible brides,
play my harmonica for scarecrows,
    & as my head clears   —nothing before me
has been charted, there's no backing up
        into tomorrow.

So I don't write poems
because each step has more to do
with stillness   — entering, balancing
dropping out of the way   with no apology
I want to talk only with the body
I want my shoulders & thighbones to move
I want to come away from the old days
                    not hardened, but wise.
I want to fall in love again
with night rain, to give comfort, to come
full circle with hope, with
                no haste & no rest

I want to sink in my axe
            & build again.

i am a man, pinwheeled from
One World to
the next

i know a man who
sang herself over.
through a typhoon ;
know a woman who
whistled his way

i am a woman, who rests
in a ≥ LIQUID SEA : womb
to womb; room to room : ONE
DREAM to the NEXT

a tree is in the cloud, whose branches
from the SOUL
praise Heaven... an eye peeks whose window
looks out from the BODY~

HOME is the PIVOT POINT, A PLACE TO BE FROM & COME BACK TO; from where the Journey UNFOLDS

THE WORD
MADE
FLESH,
& a FLOWER
OFFERED
to thee
Great
Speaker

THE FLESH
MADE
FLOWER
& a WORD
OFFERED
from
root
through
STEM to Heaven

our flesh & bone HOME! i.e. a haven; it HOME is
where you carry it, portable, like the ♥?"

David writes in
this narrow
pass: If you go this
way, the Wine might take you that fey (for you)

IX

from
HYMN FOR A NIGHT FEAST
POEMS 1979-86
(1988)

for David & Tina

"Night of darkness in the form of desire
yet liberator from the bonds of desire."
— Mahanirvana Tantra

Hymn for a Night Feast

Take the war from me.
Take the penumbra for a crossroad.
Make a parachute from our bedsheets.
Run your hand across the circuit of air
stirred by our bodies.

Take the right and wrong from me.
Take the gleam in the lamb's eye
and wear it as a gown.
Our flesh is counterfeit, fire douses water.
flame spreads the wind.

Take the smoke from my garden.
Take the river as extreme unction.
This room is moist with praise.
A crane lifts its wings
under a canopy of filtered light.

Take what is left and rock the sea.
Take the firefly, the hour hand, the iris.
Make me glorious to the world again.
Give me courage to ask
your name.

Woman Finding Herself

for Giovanna, 16th birthday

Walled flower, island
smoky with amber harbors.
Hermitage, boulevard, epistle of charm.

Your house waits in the sand
after a storm of voices
pass out of command.

Solitude, multitude.
Child in an aviary of flying stars.
Your silence is a somersault.

Success is balance
between hell's painted flower
and heaven's precise focus.

Promise to wake me
and make a face through the window
when you settle from symbols and obsidian wounds.

Promise me your address
so you and I can celebrate, as daughter
high on a warmer season.

As father
free from the madness
of weeping.

These Things Tell Me to Remember You

for Joaquin, 11th birthday

Send me a hello, young seer.
Raise a song from doubt. Name me the canyon
we once investigated. Throw the long-hidden
intuitive ace on the board of Risk.
Take your time into manhood.

Shake the leaves from Eden's tree.
Write your name in the rain.
Take the white-fire gloam of an extinguished
planet, and turn cartwheels, turn
dreamwheels, turn the arithmetic of heartbeats
        the ups and downs of seismographs
     into peaceful walks
       on the moon's other side.

It is known by mice and by tigers
by storks who leave writing over marshlands
that you can undermine anger and old imprints
of the past with slow strokes
of love, a bit of salt tide
     to burnish the woes.

There's a rhythm
to outlast society's harm, music
to begin from when the world seems left off
an anchor to weigh the boat
     when big waves threaten.

You are the vessel and the star.
You are the pulse and the hand.
You are the beauty of the seed from the flower
     in heaven which sent you.

Clown Man listening to ♪ ♪ an Underground Spring. ♪
ie: the fertile Depths of Night
fill the Belly with De Light..

"They'll Say You're on the Wrong Road If It's Your Own."
—Antonio Porchia

for Steve Sanfield

Read Tu Fu with a fire dying in the stove?
Brood over spilled wine, empty bottle, no voice
in the ringing phone as the world
slowly fills with snow?

If not poems then silence.
If not silence then the weight of snapping trees.
Or the hard fact that you're not poor
just broke — that's all.

Who to thank for the darkness?

Plug in the electric candles.
Fix the faucet that drips before the portrait
of a two men dressed as beasts in the snow.
Make plans with the angel
of destiny on your tail?

Stumble, as expected. Continue
as expected.

Connect the present
with the entire past upon which it revolves,
in one word, or even a sentence?
Don't tamper with what the Voice has to say.

The aim, destination, effort
all in one bundle. A load of wash on the head,
prayer sticks carried up a hill.
Icons, doodads. Strip them all away
and nothing's lost.

So go back to dropping the pickles
you were going to have for breakfast.
Go back to the ice-snapped trees, saw them up
for next year's warmth.

A Poem for Green

You speak of fear, silence
the nothingness of being blind
and slowly going deaf. ·

You remember yourself
as an Egyptian queen, who could turn
half-animal half-human
by rubbing an eye.

You walk me through the roses
into an orchard — you braid my hair
say, "Touch me all over."

I close my eyes
trying to know what it's like
not to see ahead.

You ask me to describe green
but my mouth won't open, my fingers
reach for your hand.
I find a harbor smooth as lacquer
and bees in an ocean of sun.

You ask me to begin a poem
about love. You say, "Start with green"
as we search for fallen pecans
with our bare toes
            at the edge of the orchard.

Faces Reflecting in Ink

1.

Sometimes the poem is a dream
never reaching print, point of darkness
in an all-seeing Eye, flicker of light
at the bottom of a well.

Sometimes the poem is healing song
sung by father to daughter after a banged knee.
Only later does that song find its
way to the page.

Sometimes the poem is a little secret
danced in the dark after a few rounds of wine
to someone you madly admire.
Once, a seventh-grader told me
        "A poem tells what a person can't say."

Sometimes the poem oscillates
between dusk and dawn and is never put down.
A place from the past that shows itself
with a flash, then ripples out beyond reach
like a blackbird's wing in the sun.

Sometimes the poem moves faster
than the eye, dodging masks, telescoping in
hidden parts of the universe.
Poems help catch a view of the Creator.
Poems open a fissure to expose the soul's geography.

They are trees making wind
stars making rays, faces reflecting in ink,
villages rocking in blue shadows of wood blocks
carved by a master designer. They are bits of mica
caught in a deer hoof, the cool print of a grasshopper
left under a dandelion.

Sometimes the poem is pure power of emotion
whirling inside us with no place to go.
Once, a friend saw a mountain lion face to face

and ran swiftly from redrock ledges, looking
for his fountain pen — not a gun.

> "Mountain lion," he wrote. "You were beautiful
> and I was not afraid."

2.

The poem begins with no end,
an anonymous dot in a Seurat painting, a forgotten
shoe lost in a canyon, a wrist watch ticking
under a lonely birch by a creek without name.

The poem is a trail song,
a story to keep things going when you're afraid
or tired or hot. Once Joaquin hiked with me
along a mesa's edge, whining — "Shade, shade."
We kept having to stop. I was getting cranky.
Finally he asked, "Why don't *you* feel the heat?"
And I answered, "Because I was born in a cave
fulla lizards!" — "Oh," he said
and asked about my life as a horned toad.
We picked up speed after that. Each footprint
became a new line, a stanza. Strength was restored
by the power of the word taking shape along the trail.
He wasn't hot anymore; the stories made us close
and the bond carried us on.

Sometimes the poem.
That's how it is. Sometimes the story or the song.
That's the way.
You can be anything in a poem — a wall or an ocean.
Like a mother giving final push to her baby
from the cave of her flesh into the light of the world.
It's the energy behind the poem that makes its form visible.
And the hand that cuts the cord to the belly
that fixes the word upon the page.

What Rite Had She?

In memory of a woman mauled
by a bear, Yellowstone

Did she sense through premonition
before she left Europe, over the Atlantic
that her fate would be
to meet a bear deep in the woods, high
in the mountains of the New World?

Perhaps in the dark marrow
of her animal self, it was already written
that she'd become prey under the new moon
far from people, blood-letting in a forest
deep among starflowers
        — an ancient fairy tale.

Perhaps the Grizzly, lured
by the scent of her menses, came forward
out of attraction — a cannibal need for love
        — a shaman ritual meant to release
            the woman's spirit
                  back into her Ancestral World.

On all fours he lumbered
toward her, then roused to lunge
while she slept — tearing her breast
        into strings, leaving the carnage
like a flare between silent evegreens.

She was only remains
when the Park Service found her
leaking back into humus — surrounded by bear prints.
As they bagged her body and lifted it away
was there confusion
in their minds — who, in their gov't uniforms
were they there to protect
           trees   rivers   bears
               tourists?

And how would they explain

the loss of a daughter to parents in Switzerland
over long-distance telephone?
        — that America is still wild with bears
who, like their Old World cousins
        sometimes walk upright here in the New
and rise to the blood-thrill of the senses
        dreaming the dreamer who sleeps
            alone in the woods?

Eating her flesh
        to partake of her power, releasing spirit
from body in ritual kill (as ancient
        tribesmen once downed the bear itself, eating
its body to release its spirit
        in another, more fertile world;
and to assure its return
        into this one forever)

Ursus Horribilis,
        where now do you disappear to
after the kill? Into the darkest part
of our continent, down again
        peacefully on all fours?
        — and that woman
          what rite
            had she, in your
                Grizzly world?

Reading *Ghost Tantras* Waiting for a Night Flight

for Michael McClure

Newlyweds deboard
from Istanbul, jackhammers rage
at the tarmac. Two French ladies
roll up red stockings
and converse in b flat. A breakdancer
plugs himself in and does a chiropractic flip.
An eyelid moves, a face frowns, an airplane
lands in the rain.

Lovers kiss
and part their hair in black mirrors.
The ashtray lady empties waste
under Federico Garcia's face.
Men work crosswords; blue lights reach
toward the metaphysical bay.
Behind the *Chronicle*'s open headlines
is a statue in thought.
Inside the statue, a complicated heart.
Inside the heart, a concealed wing.

Arrivals and departures flash
on the screen. Kerosene roar vibrates
windowpanes. Yes,
      "BODY EATS BOUQUETS
             OF THE EAR'S VISTA. EACH BLOT OF SOUND
                IS A BUD OR A STAHR."
And who are we, all of us
but GHOSTS lifted from crosswords,
tantras of pure sound
      fastening seatbelts
          as karma calls us on?

San Francisco International Airport

Down the Night like whitewater, to try to Realize the Quest isn't planned, but Given as we go...

Nothing to Reason, stands to Reason, All is Metaphor for Something Else.

Each presence is Luminous & Escaping. Every gesture a Shadow from another Reality. The Road Narrows between acceptance & Disbelief.

"I write to prism the Air & give back our Secret Shape"

1. In Ihuatzio a girl with ½ smile hands me a flying fish

2. On the trail to Tzintzuntzan I find a deerprint glowing in the dark

3. In Santo Domingo a clown with red handprint on his face climbs a ladder to the moon.

XI:2:85

Tzintzuntzan Mexico: over & over we write the same poem, discover a molten zero in the face of the sun, lift brush with toes, obedient to pure blood pulse spawned by dreams.

Biting the Chill

At 40 below
in the new village center
the world is a windowpane, edged
with condensation of weary men, dogs
with ice spears around
        lower jaws; the rattle
                of generators.

Fox man jokes
promiscuously about the Moravian
preacher's second wife;
        northern lights coil, teletype
luminous bouquets
that disappear, and recompose themselves
as sound, a pictorial echo
        in the ear.

Young Eskimos
break dance in the gym, the old shaman
(videotaped by reporters
        for public broadcasting) gnaws beavertail
and tunes his walrus-gut drum.

Grandkids spread themselves
on linoleum floors, watching *Dynasty*
from satellite tv; or listen to cassettes
        of ZZ Top, ears plugged
                to arctic tundra blasters.

Back from the hunt
Wassilie cleans grass from the stomach
of a slaughtered moose, warns
        the youngsters, "Don't stand
in the doorway, unless you want
        your future to pass you by."

Ghost squalls whistle
through corrugated eaves. Inside,
        the table is spread with sinew
        baleen and bone. Outside,

in the dead of winter
    the air is moving a thousand
      miles per hour.

Upper Nushagak, Alaska
13:IV:86

Preparing the Nets at New Stuyahok

Break the law!
Climb the windy forefront and
burn in the snow.

Chant the oldtime song
and melt like ice
off Nunivak.

Mend and lower the nets
of revolution.

Let the men who say
bombing makes sense be served
infinity's harsh illusion.

Let them die
in the distance between the countries
they have eyes on.

Aleknagik

Wake from spring nap, swollen eyed
swallowing dream ash from Mt. Pavlof, mosquito crushed
in last summer's morass

News of terrorists
bombing terrorists over shortwave . . .

Madonna listening to *Revelation*
with her Eskimo prince, Kristi adjusting
her earrings in an ice pane . . .

Old Uppa shaking with laughter
in the heat of his sweat lodge (a wolf pack's
whereabouts divined in the steam)

Raven, shifty footed
on an abandoned fish rack . . .

Yes, I want to run faster than caribou
leave wolfprints written in snow, pierce my ear
with the thermometer stopped below zero

Follow snowgeese to Anaktuvuk
circle Maui in a Lamborghini, come back
to your village

Feast on stories, lovemake every different way
swim like king salmon, leap through whitewater
never get my fill!

1 + 1 + 1 + 1 + 1 + 1 = 1

for Nanao

No east no west no south
no north no center no space
that surrounds

No word no sound no wing
no stone no ground
no door no room

No star no flesh no bone
no pain no flotsam of human centuries
no crack of whip nor shot of gun

No womb no ocean
no phallus no cloud no bicycle
no boat no oar no wave

No bomb no wind
no flower no ash circling from fire
no radio nothing named

No beginning no end no middle
nothing latched
no sonnet battling free form no game

Nothing won or lost
no bible no tarot no veda no gilgamesh
no step just taken nor about to be made

No vapor no shine no darkness
no crime no meaning under the tongue
no blame no automobile no tomb no skyscraper

Nothing dirty nothing clean
no this nor that
no be or not to be

No me no you no them no us
no brain no body no arms to reach
nor finger to explode

No everythig no nothing
no yes no no.

Great Circle Route, 2:V:86

Madrigal, An April Morn

There is a net between your breasts.
A net of sighs and fields mowed with blades of steel.
There is an owl who flies over you.
An owl whose eyes bleed and who never remembers names.
There is an ear at your side.
An ear that hears whispers of other lovers
who've come to you on mornings like these.

There is soil between your teeth.
Soil of buried seeds and vanished towns, of hidden
letters and deaths of ones near.
There is a highway that connects us.
A highway through trample of rain
and mirrored canyons at the break of day.

There is this you, this me
who fold into the deepest blossom
with no fear of night's undertow, no dark hedge
behind which to pretend.

There is a river of dust, a mirage
of silence to begin the world.
There is your face and mine.
There are these bodies never here for long,
these breasts and private parts ready to sing.
This innocence, this lust, this pain we hold.

There is this you, this me
who sleep inside shadows, who rise
from under a wing to grasp a hand through a flame
and discover someone waiting, whose flesh
reveals the Body inside the bodies of everyone.

Here, Give Me Your Hand

Tonight, the warmth of spring
covers the land. A horse in the field
whinnies namelessly. Something
in the sky I never noticed before
answers back.

As we sleep
a greatness circles the body.
Wide nets of stars move in and out
of place. The poplars light themselves
like candles under the moon.

I am weightless
in your arms. Our bones shine
through the skin's transparence.
We are sleepers, we are lovers carried
from one dream to another.

When we awake
the apricot trees have erupted
into flowers. The mirror, the horse
the oranges on the table
have all changed places.

Everything is joined this morning.
Today is the first day of the world.
Here, let me draw you a city
without fright.
Here, give me your hand
      let me walk you to the center
      of a Circle of Light.

It is Not the You

It is not the you of long lines.
The windwashed you, the rainblown you of Manhattan,
the exasperated you walking the streets of old Kathmandu.
It is not the you of short lines, of arctic light
splintering below an airplane wing over the St. Elias range.
Nor the offshore you rowing backwards into reefs
of solidified language.
It is not this I recall as you.
Not the past participle of mist behind a rainbow.
Nor the pre-destined verb circling lost cargo underwater
or a village beneath a desert in Mongolia.
But the all at once you.
The you of unraveled stockings with sudden hellos
at my afternoon door, the exactly-centered you,
a hummingbird at the mouth of a scarlet gila.
The tequila you in the rain at the opera.
The you of tempered crystal on a shelf by a Chinese novel.
The you of mascara eyes fixed upon two lovers
in a blizzard, or birds whose beaks pry through
phosphorescence of dead meat on a highway at night.

It is this that is you.
The you of melancholy proposals and unmarried flings.
The dance-shoe you whose half-life privately spirals inward.
The you in a lightning field after sunset
or under a cottonwood whose leaves have just become
the mosaics of St. Sophia.
It is this that is you.
The warm feather, the rewritten lines
the print of amaryllis in dark peat, the quarrel over tea,
over the rotation of comets. The catered dinner
eaten with borrowed silverware, the unhooked blouse
beneath a flaming chandelier, the bright veins
of pomegranate, the cold bottles of perfume.

It is this that is you.
The you of frozen shorelines
and mountains vibrating with flowering bamboo.
The you of no middle way, the chameleon you.
The Old World you listen to in coils of deep-sea fossil,

in a smoking cobweb, an indigo shadow
in the center of a dead volcano.
The you of super novae and disassembled horizons,
of undivided highways suspended over blank canyons.
The circular landscape whose edges curl inward.
The fish whose bones are pressed into vertical layers
of igneous walls surrounding a nocturnal camp.
It is this that is you.
It is this that wakes somewhere else
up the street down the block between the sheets
above the fog inside the lamp.
It is this that sends me on a parallel path
through the reeds into ultraviolet heat, storming cinemas
into the waterfall for a long-distance call.

It is this that is you.
The de Kooning you, the Rothko you, the O'Keeffe you
of black iris and headlines wrapped in plastic
on a doorstep in the rain.
The idyllic you, the magnetized thread
between freedom and silence, the phantom you facing east
from Soho. The lucent you, the perfume you.
The you whose heart is rain which does not taste.
The you whose book is beside mine.
The you of wounded love and solitary hiding.
The strong arm you, the nonchalance you.
The you of no backwards glance, the you of aurora borealis.
The Schönberg you, the hot boulevard you.
The you of no punctuation, the you of weeks and dates
and seasons and years that have combined
neither by chance nor configuration
to make you nobody else but you.

New York City / Rome / Istanbul

Rasa Lila, Kanchipuram

Saw you
in a flight of bees through
the rice sprinkled door of Kali's shrine.

Saw you
in springtime thunderbolt void
wave splashing the diamond shore of Shiva's beach.

Saw you
turn in sleep, transparent in timeless
consciousness, swimming through the world's tricks.

Saw you
at the balcony, watching the undoings of men
body smoking, hair falling like water.

Saw you
empty dreaming eyes of holy trance
arms reaching through the painted haze of reality.

Saw you
and heard the unborn singing
as I wrapped myself into you.

Saw you
take from me a key, a ring, a saber, a mirage
a bouquet of milky light.

Saw you
and saw through you, a mirror
a clock, a child sleeping at the end of night.

Tamil Nadu, India
1982

I Am Not Thinking Anything

I am not thinking anything
though you think I am thinking something.
I am riding the fine dust that floats
past your door.
I am waiting for children not yet born.
Someone is forging my name to make a tiny window
into the next world.
But I am not thinking anything
though you think I am thinking something.

I am a wish circling
tomorrow's lost forever.
I am a cat cutting across your best laid plans.
I am on the true path of exile
with a girl who says she can't dance.
And, really, I am doing nothing more
than taking her home for the night, even though
you and I have taken a few vows.
I am doing nothing more than starting a rumor
with no other desire than to remain faithful
to beauteous exits, to remembered alleys.
Even though you think I am thinking something
I am not thinking anything.

I am a shoal of barracuda
untied from a reef, the light of a vanished star
figuring a course through a canyon.
There are camellias in my hand.
I am on a bridge with a jazz trumpet, waiting for you.
Here is a gangplank, there is a ferry boat.
You can see for yourself
that I am not thinking anything
though you think I am thinking something.

Old Beast Self

Trees named
flowers named
continents named
bombsites memorialized
roadsigns quadrupled, thunder rerouted
lightning detoured
weather televised, music canned
dogmeat canned, uranium canned
Walt Disney frozen
Billy the Kid's body stolen
outer space wired
blackbirds poisoned
Popeye painted on warheads
electrocution sanctioned
phone wires tapped, geysers tapped
volcanoes monitored
terrorism mass-marketed
crime popularized, burglary syndicated
lies memorized, death squads okayed
rainforests mapped
fir trees under contract, inlets earmarked
cows branded, knowledge booked
books shredded, time put into ticks
ticks digitalized
good will fossilized, mythology vandalized
honesty scrutinized
planet light eyed by marketing executives
chins, noses, breasts re-arranged in surgery rooms
bodies mugged, straights plugged
flags pinned to the other side of the moon
scientists, poets, nuns silenced
hearts transplanted
satellites re-paving the night sky
earthworms boxed and sold
crocodiles skinned
counselors, therapists, mail-course astrologers
dissecting peoples' lives

HELP

I want my body back
I want my old beast self
I want a voice that sings high-altitude clear
I want to live without being watched
smile without being choked, bathe myself unmonitored
sleep without someone ringing my number!
I want to make love
without being told how to do it, what to feel
how to wake next morning
what time of day it is, who's in the World Series
who's winning the latest war
who's been left in purgatory
and not gone to heaven
S T O P

Let me lose myself for once
Let me see who I am
Empty pockets of driver's license, spare change
social security, draft card, secret phone numbers
fake student ID, Visa, Mastercharge!
I want to eat without additives, die without preservatives
I want to rise from the world's debris
wipe the rusted mirror, have a feast!
I want to feel my body naked
wet with storm, stuck with pollen, tanned
with meteor fire, soused with cold rain!
I want to pass through Halley's tail
bloom, shake my mane, stretch the stiff joints
roll in the mustard, kick my heels
silver the dry wash with rafts of light
unbloody the ocean, unsmoke the stack
undo the noose, unframe the framed
let loose the shadows
lick the salt from the world's tears
No flags!
No heads ruling hearts!
No dirty clothes piled in the closet
No bomb hatch on the horizon!

Let me flood through the gate
slide into you
embrace without could be's.
I want it
a hundred times the first time
I want it slow
in the open, luminous
sourceless, as books never
tell it, as vision never witnesses it
I want it blessed
by the brightest angel
I want it in the clover, in the clouds
with the furious taste
of electricity, with silence left
in my lungs
with my windshield steamed   I want it
high on a greenwet wave
and the whole world with me, out   in
back through the narrow vent
of birth
then to sleep to drift to wake!
beckoned by no absence
collective and unnamed,   feathered
horned
soft pawed
haloed
bloodsong in the veins
birdwhistle in the artery
fin in surfspray

I want it
heavenknowswhere, I want
my body back
I want my Old Beast Self!

A Message From Han Shan

Dead leaves whirl through my mind.
Under bare cottonwoods, I listen to Bach
    play a fugue via satellite radio.
Then, the news, reporting $180,000 wasted
by the State Department after World War II
studying a plan for interstellar
migration   — to house battered refugees
                    in outer space.

In the bathtub a dying cricket
sings her marooned plea. Beyond the peaks
two fighter planes scour the ridge
in mock dog fights.

After dark, I look up
into the stars, and realize *Alpha Centauri*
is the nearest one.   It would take a thousand
centuries to reach it   while Han Shan's retreat
            is less than an eye-wink away.

That Chinese hermit
used a cloud for a pillow, woke in silence
under a cinnamon tree.
He had no clear-cut trail up Cold Mountain
and taught that if one's surroundings
are quiet, all cravings can be
cut down   (A Bach fugue can be learned
              from a cricket in a bathtub).

Tonight, I chop parsley
while an innocent family commits suicide
to keep from getting gunned down
by enemies once friends,
turned against them by big-power nations.

Nobody wants to take blame.
The world swings like a pendant over a well.
I think of cold wars, hot wars
and Cold Mountain, remembering a man
　　　who returned to the very Center
　　　　　　leaving no trace of himself
　　　between highrock cliffs.

Han Shan's place
might have been myth, and my place
facing the arroyo, shaken by sonic fighters
　　　might tomorrow be memory.
Yet, I go forward through sidetracks
　　　　　　and upheaval.

Tonight
there are mass executions
while I fall into sleep. A cold moon
rises behind the gate.
　　　At 3 a.m. I wake to a line of smoke
a little above the fields.
Already the horses are kicking their trough
　　　　　　impatient for dawn.

When the sun finally rises
the smoke still hangs.　　Clear,　white
　　　from fires burning through the night.
Thin,　curled
　　　　　like a scroll from centuries past
　　　　　like a message
　　　　　　　　from Han Shan.

Tesuque, New Mexico, 1982

True Love

True love
forms zero, begins
and ends without declaration
sings the body Yes
asks nothing
in return.

True love
permits light
between storm, fears
no twirling wobble
from which
to rise.

True love
says it all
with the blink of an eye
without speech
without miracle
True love
becomes wine
from its own water.

TRUE LOVE
forms a ZERO, Begins
& ends without Declaration
Sings the body YES
asks nothing
in Return.

TRUE LOVE
permits light
between STORM, fears
no TWiRLing wobble
from Which
to Rise.

TRUE LOVE
says it all
with the Blink of an Eye
without Speech
without MiRaCLe
TRUE Love
Becomes wine
from its OWN WATeR.

A Poem for Light

1.

Dumbstruck light.
Light of opening roses.
Busy revolutionary light
seeding the body.
Light of questions
turned upside down in midflight.
Reflected light
from tarns and axes.
Light inside the ear that pretends
not to hear.
Female light, escaping
from streams, onto roads
into oceans and taverns.
Light from the body
as it begins its prayer.
Wheatfields of light
waving inside bread on the table.
Light made into active horizons.
Slow moving wicks of flame
forming nouns and possessives
under shirts and blouses.
Amorous light
penetrating the delicate tangle.
Light scattered into figures
bent into Arabics.
Captive light webbed
through steel and malachite.
Light of the flicker, winging
without regard for borders.
Absolute light
erupting from pockets
of spare change.
Dream of light,
when shadow parts
from body.

2.

Maker of light
who hides inside us.
Intersections of light
 in New York or Nairobi.
Light from the heels of a posse
galloping across a desert
to the music of Vivaldi.
Light germinating
from the mouth of honeysuckle.
Light gnarled in roots
and graves, spinning up
from confessionals and emergency rooms.
Light of desire, light
of t*erra incognita.*
Light from the side of Christ
nailed to the sky
and Saint Thomas doubting.
Hallucinogen light.
Light of Hassids praying.
Light of dervishes spinning.
Light of broken-shoed preachers
in airports, on avenues.
Light from cities holy
and cities absurd
each in their own way
shining.

3.

Light spawned
by the breast nursing flesh
formed within, and hands
reaching out.
Heart beating light
wave rocking light.
Nice girls censoring their light.
Lasers, candles, smudgepots
green auroras shivering with light.
Shoes filled with stockings of light.

Alleys burning with light.
Silks and gunbarrels
wine bottles
and movie houses
giving off
light.

4.

Light from bomb hatches
opening in attack.
Battles fought with light.
 Refugees running
from light.
Gods and devils pulling punches
with light.
 Scientists programming light.
Light in the insane asylum.
Matadors weeping
in arenas of light.
Victor]ara's light.
Pablo Neruda's light.
White light around the convertible
of Kennedy's final handwave.
Red light from the eye
of Chief Joseph.
Amplified light from the guitar
of Bob Marley
Light spilling from Aquino's body
on the runway, from Silkwood's tires
on the highway.
Martin Luther King's light.
Light out of the back
of]ohn Lennon's head.
Light caught in the whirlpool
center of Janis]oplin.
Light between the lines
of Che Guevara's diary.
Light barricaded and frozen
into shadows of panic.
Light distorted and used

to execute.
Human bonfires burning
in requiems.
Human pyres sending spirals
of light back to the sun.
Barbed wire light.
Trenches of light filled
with marines and guerillas.
Light that marries
for money.
Light that stands on its tiptoes
to see behind the window.
Light of the unpaid dowry.
Light of the wife's kerosene soaked
body set to fire by inlaws.
Nests of light hatched
by storks and quail.
Seams of light between cracks in the ghetto.
Light in prisms
racing across rice fields.
Monsoon light
drenching the world's famine.
Light busting its ass
to make a point.
Electric light.
Stained glass light.
Light of Turner.
Light caught in parachutes.
Light ricocheting off temple domes
in Pondicherry and Karachi
in Sitka and Varanasi.
Architecture of pure light .

5.

Light made passionate
by Michelangelo and Chagall.
Light in places
that have never seen light.
Polarized light when two people fight.
Light that blasts us

to Kingdom Come.
Texas barroom two step light.
Tesuque pueblo rain dance light.
Light between the rungs
of Jacob's ladder, in the hairline curve
of a Venus Flytrap, in the ballet
of jellyfish tentacles.
Molecules of light reassembling
before bed in the mirror.
Light bubbling into a cry, a kiss
a pregnant mother's sneeze.
Light on the balastrade at the foot
of a stairway.
Shipwrecked light, toadstool light,
light from the burro's heehaw.
Sea divers bringing up barrels
of light. Rusted light
virgin light, mineral light
thrown away light.
Atomic light
fossilized into cold layers
of stone.
Light from a marksman's delivery.
Light that dies framed
and caged behind bars.
Cool light surrounding the magnolia.
Snakeskins of light
blowing across the prairie.
Light remembering freedom
with a sigh.
Bodies of light
created from alphabets.
Light between us
and within.

6.

Light eternal, suspended
like a dream around the body.
Rivers of light, bafflements of light
that I must cross.

Light inside the hands waiting for a shake.
Waterfalls of light washing
us back into wild systems
of thought.
Light of continents at peace
instead of war.
Shooting stars over seaports
and deserts, over
cities and farms.
Light eternal, suspended
like a dream around the body.
Light between us
and within.

7.

Collective light,
light of our bodies remembering
their essence.

5 ~.
No.
1990

In Sleep we
Dream To Find en-
Trance inside The
Possibility we Deny.
Tongve Rolls Bakwards into
BODY Cirls up !
a Maze an enormous Eye
innside

In Sleep we Remember
WHAT it IS to be Awake.

We OPen the
Garden's Gate, &
Langvage
follow to thee Mouth
of the Cave.

X.

from
SHADOW PLAY:
POEMS 1987-1991
(1992)

for Susan

"I want to be with those who know secret things
or else alone."
— Rainer Maria Rilke

Shadow Play

Doubt fuels us,
faith keeps the body in place.
No word approximates the fire
that shapes the wind.

Silence surrounds us
like pounding rain.

We rise into a world
of heated verbs, sacrifice
the alphabet on a moving bough
of leaves.

What we write is shadow play,
pollen sifting
from the body's tree.

I See You in a Dream

I am amazed.
I see you in a dream, and you are entertaining me.
We are both very young. Everything is in color
except the two parentheses
floating slightly above, like fragments of vegetation
in a Max Ernst painting.
And then I write a poem that has nothing to do
with the dream. I scribble extra fine
fade proof lines into my notebook, on bridges,
inside tunnels. I sit in a cathedral
sharpening pencil shavings into my pants cuff
while security guards fondle their walkie talkies.

It's a perfect day
just to be nobody, to examine the ghost
inside my eye or the periwinkle bobbing its face
to the whoofing pile driver three blocks away.
There's a nice shade of green on the eyelids
of the waitress who spills my coffee
watching the guy out the window behind his easel
making the invisible a possibility.

Life is full of details.
The present tense of past history, the dreamy
substance of philosophy, a dog walking its owner
past glassy storefronts filled with powdered
antlers and seahorses upside down in a bowl.
And I am just stepping along,
part of the scenario, fighting off the urge
to wear a green cape and pink jockstrap
when my daughter brings her friends to meet me.
But anyway, listening to the former Miss America
get sent up for grand larceny
is just as good.

I love the big city hall
so phallic and art deco, all lit up at night
when you drive in from the Canadian side.
It's so good to feel free — but I get dizzy often.
I lost my equilibrium at Niagara Falls.

I got sick on the Eiffel Tower.
But I'm shaping up in my old age.
I want to see the Liberace sequin collection
and catch Khrushchev pounding his shoe
in the Toledo Wax Museum.
I'll probably finish the day walking up the street
across the lake to see the latest exhibit, maybe
end up eating bonbons in front of the screen
remembering the big scribbly heads
of Jean Dubuffet.

Then I'll brew some tea
and fall asleep. There'll be noises upstairs.
Lovers gently wooing each other, making
seismographic waves in the park across the street.
I'll set my wristwatch, dream of notes
like Charlie Parker. The windows
will steam. Sun will rise above the theater
and trolley cars, over river docks
where Chinese shopping bag ladies
and meteorologists in plastic raincoats
and the Quaker Oats looking man under the clock tower
with a French Canadian nun
will be talking in perfect circles.

Yes, it's already morning.
Twenty-four hours have passed. I'm licking
this closed. I just wanted you to know I'm glad
for the new bridge, and the way they fixed the airport.
It's so convenient. And the styles they're wearing
make me think we live in a really big city.

One last thing.
You know when the colored lights came on
that time at the falls, how the water
actually seemed to be stopped, not going up or down?
Well, it's similar to a shift in color
when you paint — how an effect is created in the eye
and what is seen, though it is really moving,
appears to be absolutely still.

I remember
how we blinked at each other, how everybody
around us was just shadows.
There was a big burst of flashbulbs
and for a moment we saw sixteen Japanese men
against a granite rail, each holding
an empty rubber camera case looped around his wrist.
Then it was dark again,
full of mist coming up from below
and the sound of airplanes flying above.

Remember?
I was starting to tell you
how we were both very young, and you
were entertaining me. It was at the beginning.
Everything was black and white, as I recall
except the two parentheses
or maybe I am mistaken, and we are not
those same people.

Niagara Falls, 1987

This Language Isn't Speech

This language isn't speech.
It's a blossom in the doorway slowly opening,
one reverberation
     mating with another —heat of a rose
salt smoke from a sea wave.
Something inside the flesh that trembles
     as the center shifts between us.

It is very quick isn't it?

This montage of soundwaves
describing silence. Question mark inscribed
in a storm of pollen.

I give you a floating island,
one eye to see, another to feel. You arch your back,
shake gold leaf into a shower of Off Minor.

This language is a horizon
terraced into a ladder that spins
into a blade of light, and drugs the darkness
     with its brilliant stem.

Desire smiles in all directions at once.

It's the magnet in your pocket.
It's two minerals in their proper field of glow.
It's the summer tanager in silver chamisa.
It's the handprint in the sun
    bringing forth the names of children.

Think of wings pushing through shoulders.
Think of drinking the compass to become a map.
Think of rain pouring from an eave
with no cloud above, a wet alphabet trembling
inside the spine. Or to escape through the letter O
     to be naked inside the curve of an S.

You're the symbol for what you write.
    Pumpkin blossom, dewdrop, mica

a stone-pecked bird inside the chest
    of a star-headed man.
You're the barefoot girl in a mirrored cove
who trims the leaves to greet the sun.
You're a cyclone breathing phosphorescence
       into space between the hands
          thirsting at the gate.

You open the door, I see you part way
     —taste the jazz of what's begun
form a lasso of stars   and laugh
that you are real —that webs of blood and crystal
begin what we speak   or that what we speak
is more like silk . . . slowly sliding back and forth
over two bodies undressed in the stillness
    there in the shine,
       there   very deep.

I Saw Kit Carson Still Alive

"He was a likable soft-spoken man
whose exploits contributed much toward
the settlement of the west"
— *Encyclopedia Britannica*

I saw Kit Carson still alive
cruising the reservation, driving through Window Rock,
up over the hill towards Naschitti and Biklabito,
the consumer producer vending obsolescence, measuring people
in units of profit, reading the desert
as one vast print out.

I saw him step from an Eagle,
the BIA official from back east, looking for points
to advance his career. He was the relocation agent
eying hillsides, surveying canyons, planning
quick-development housing, calling long distance
to line up friends for under-the-table contracts.

I watched him at Black Mesa.
I saw him at Shiprock, pulling the brake at Colonel Sanders,
cleaning his carbine on a formica table, bulldozing peach trees,
handing out free radioactive mine tailings,
telling the people of Paguate, "Here, make your adobes,
build new foundations."

He was in Tohatchi and Many Farms,
marching schoolkids through freezing rain
to salute the flag. He was holed up in a town named after Cortez,
the liquor retailer, sitting up late designing billboards
showing a tight-jeaned woman beckoning men
with an open blouse and outstretched arm
holding a bottle of tokay.

He swiveled in his chair, downshifted into third,
rode a glass elevator high above the world
three-thousand miles away. I saw him slip into his saddle,
unfold his maps, spit dust outside Paradise Disco,
pass out Bibles under a portable placard saying: *First Indian
Free Will Full Gospel Pre Millennium Church of God.*

He cocked his hat, timed his watch;
his infrared cigarette burned down into the night.
He talked low, made camp, built a hogan-shaped saloon
with his brother-in-law a hundred yards
from the reservation boundary.
He was the one who grabbed Mrs. Yazzie by her velveteen collar
and pushed her into the snow when she came to save
her husband from another night of drinking.

I saw him, Kit Carson
working gears and levers way up high behind the scoop
of his three-million dollar power shovel,
training men to dig up the land, trade in the old ways,
mine coal, get a job with Sacred Mountain Electric.

He was the powerplant industrialist
breaking for lunch at Best Western Inn.
He polished his spurs, got a shave, had a girl sent up
to his room. He was there generating sulfurous haze
over cornfields and rivers, spilling waste
into drinking holes and village wells.
He was busy manufacturing electricity for Los Angeles
and Phoenix, the gambling halls of Vegas,
the used-car lots and nuke sites.

I saw him down low
behind the tinted windows of his Cougar
secretly jotting notes for his PhD, writing a book
to size things up; in Tuba City, in Round Rock
he was there bribing Indian leaders, buying off tribal officials
to pave inroads for corporate bosses to confuse
the Athapaskan grandmother and steal her land.
He was getting rich on radioactive disposal, on Pampers,
on Lethal 1080 used to wipe out Coyote.

He kicked dust from his hooves,
climbed Defiance Plateau in his four wheeler,
had a picnic at Washington Pass, looking down into wide expanse
of red desert and brown mesas, he spied through field glasses
and licked his chops. On the highways,
in the bars   —it was 1864 1878 1964 1989.

I saw Kit Carson,
   he was still there, doing his thing.

Shiprock, New Mexico
1986-1989

At Wovoka's Ghostdance Place

I blow dandelion heads
across Wovoka's ghostdance place.
Hear tractors whine through alfalfa fields.
Hear the call of deer continuing history.
Feel moment to moment
the river's bend, shift of jetstream
bringing rain, heat in snakes
moving across highway.

I bow to magpies
drinking in light from dark
old sediment, to grass waving
with resilience, to the force of everything
here long before us.

The way it was
and how it'll come back to be,
yielding, yielding
to all of it
that's yielded me.

Walker River, Nevada
Vernal Equinox, 1990

To a Young Student, Blizzard Hill

Turn deep
where no path leads.
Let the snow bank melt into a wing.
Give flame to the pencil's wick.
Make papyrus boat, make time to sail.

Follow backwards
the string to the cave's mouth.
Know the dark is gentle
behind open teeth.
Be brave, be brief.

You'll leave your mark
without resumes, in crossings
that never wear thin
inside the architecture
of human concern.

Be passionate, be
precise in the sowing, be wise
be *there*
wherever you go.

7:3: MOXIE & NICOLAS POINTING OUT "WOLF CONSTELLATION," −22 + WIND CHILL...

9:3: TO KOLIG-ANEK—flying over TUNDRA, SAW those "HIDING SHAMAN" IVAN'S WIFE WAS TALKING ABOUT

MARY'S MASKS MOUTH VOMITS HEADED OUT & KAYAK TO SEA see.

10/3: flite into ALEKNAGIK. The ½ froze lake, & SMOKE WISPS FROM STEAM LODGES

12 March: in arctic sunless "ness"

Thinking: "Dont give up, give inn... give OUT!

North Country, A Sketch

Snow is whirling
across the tables, the cake, the flowers.

But the bride isn't eager to walk the aisle.
She lights a fire to flags and laws

And buries a knife
in the snow-filled sleigh.

Her belly is huge with refusal.
The rebel in her rebuttons memory's torso.

She's round and beautiful, she's shaking
under the crackling sweep of the aurora.

Her fists curl inward,
darkness fills the blizzard of sleep.

She will learn to carve ice, spit at the stars
and begin to drink.

Meltwater fills the wolverine's tracks,
snow crystals pile at the window.

It should be spring, not winter.

"But the loon's been shot from the sky,"
she writes

"If not for this, I'd breathe gently,
a new road in the night."

For Hasya

— birth of first grandchild
3 August 1989

The pathway shines!

May the power of breath, love,
courage be with you.

From your mother's house
you slip out to fill the gate,

To become visible,
truly here.

Breathe, little one
rearrange the world with your smile.

Bring rain to the garden,
carry with you always

The light
from which you've taken hold.

Remind us that we are an echo
forever arriving into the dream called life.

Praise the Mystery
as together we swim this stream.

Let us live fully, and truthfully
as we begin our return

To the House
from which all things are born.

Threnody for Chama Ruiz

I know the breath that parents our bodies,
rebellion's dark paradise that explodes in cathedrals.
I know the howl that feeds the inevitable revolution,
the hallucinating eye of the volcano,
the monarchy of delirium.

I know we spoke in solar stanzas, carved our names
on a branching rainbow, identified the flora
and held to truths. I know a diamond's brightness
in fossil darkness.

I know you lie in the unmade bed
and stir my morning coffee. That you dazzle
the battalion with your open book, that you
are reading my Upper Arcana.

I know the veil has been lifted,
that you've gone to heaven to mix up the angels,
placed weightless cairns
that lead back to the garden.

I know I'll find you sleeping in the dream
that began us. That the children look up
when a cloud passes.

I know I knew you as a body
and now I know you
no matter what you are wearing.

The Body Burns Strong It Wavers
It Loosens It Dims It Flares Back
It Extinguishes Itself & is Born Somewhere Else

To pass away, no
to leave the world, die, depart, no
because even in the deepest canyon of your leaving
under the oaks, in a meadow, beneath the foam
of colliding seas, you come back . . .

As a seed, raw light
around an embryo, vibratory music inside the solar
plexus, or understream in the song
of creekwashed stones,
you come back . . .

To ambush empty space, dance
in glacial corridors, to touch hurried lines of workaday
women, embrace a child after a dream, or rise
from a stag's antlers as wisps of steam,
you come back . . .

To obliterate the squares, set fire to the corners,
smooth the devouring darkness,
to answer through a broken wing
or in the keyboard jazz of midnight swing,
you come back . . .

To call from across the river, yes
to pass away, no.

To the Burmese Military Regime

I smuggle out a tooth inside my ear,
smuggle out fear, cross the line with protest monks,
protest students, workers who chant down
machine-gun fire in tracts of hardwood forest
up for grabs on the world market.

I see Buddha's rusted upturned hand
begging right attitude; farmers ready to take stand;
citizens proud —like aged banyan trees
sending down roots to destroy stale foundations
of old temples that nursed them into existence.

I smuggle in seeds and medicine,
smuggle in truth,
pull "revolt" from "revolution"
        — send it, too.

Karen People's Liberation Camp
Ba Wa Ley, Burma 1989

Night is An Upside Down SHIP Starring You & Me.

the present
WRAPS the
around the
FUTURE, the past
& keeps on going
until all things
Are part of
What has Been,
isn't & ABout
to Be

who was
it, took
my HAND
thru a Moving STAR,
gladdened My staff
with Her Bouquet?

Fragments from Insomnia

Sing if sorrow fills you.
Keep in mind the colors of Kandinsky,
the political body of Frida, stars whose tongues
are ablaze and make green the olives in jars,
the grass between hooves of horses.

For a second — just a second
we are here.

So fill your teeth with dust.
Eat and eat and eat — until the horizon is clear.
Plant a seed, keep your promises,
seek the dream that sounds your name.

What's to be certain about
except the radiance of shooting stars, lives lived
in foggy rings around the moon,
hammered gold in the throat
of a storm — a wide open sail, the wind
upon it, and tonight
tonight — how far
inside am I.

Lyric Written With Both Hands

Yes to alchemy
transforming names back into trees;
No to concrete eating green

Yes to imagination's endless abyss
ever luminous and creating;
No to fake masters of ceremony
misdirecting life's play

Yes to deadwood piled around fields fair,
to water refilling aquifers;
No to faith without room for doubt

Yes to the galaxy unweighted by greed;
No to minds with rusty rakes
fouling the planet, pest-spraying the wide awake

Yes to Adam created from Eve
recognizing himself in every she;
No to rage falsified into smiles,
to money culture that bribes the child

Yes to mystery that raises the wave;
No to dictators stopping spring

Yes to the uncapitalized i inside the Eye
that bigly sees the power of small;
No to sawmill smoke from cut-down dreams,
timber strewn over muddy lakes

Yes to the prayer primordially there
all the time in the breath

Yes to the yes that brings us to sea
Yes to this moment, our selves
    one Self, the body free.

This Poem for Maria Still Inside

Is waiting like a drowsy woman
to be made into the exact proportion she has dreamed.
Right voice, perfectly toned flesh. Unspeakable
values that would stop men cold
and find them all guilty.

Last summer
hoeing the ground, opening
water gates, I tried.
Last Christmas, when the garden suddenly
warmed and the ground was full
of considerable opposites
I almost tamed the poem.

Walkways burned
with the moon's cold reflection.
The mirror shook and filled with exquisite
lavender. Through work and distress,
war and grim solitude
every good intention kept intact.

Inside the spine
it's still there. It begins to tickle
the throat, and lays itself out   way out
in the warm saki, in the pink and silver sashimi
at a little joint called Taki's where I write . . .

Please be still. And wait.
Brother to sister, we are
so much closer
              and so unknown.

Vernal Feast:
luminous mem-
brane fiery deep
with PACIFIC
MIGRA-
TIONS:

I eat thee, Scent of Birth,
Star ☩ Bound Navigator,
whose god-flesh melts in
mouth's heat.. Totem ani-
mal, you taste of twilight's
Honeycomb. Fish Bright with
Planet Light. Opulent Dream
that feeds EACH line I ∴!
WRITE°

Journal Entry, West of Reno

Not such a bad day.
Won seventeen twenty in the slots.
Received hard cash for old Gurdjieff books.
Offered blue flames to a smiling virgin.
Bought gooseberries in a Paiute smoke shop.
Pressed Johnny Jump Ups into new notebook.
Decorated stone with ribbons
for meditative shadow flutter.
Raised kitchen window to sound of silence
between bird calls.
Read about swallowtails and genebanks.
Discovered it's not just the tip,
but the whole fingernail that grows.
Bathed in hot springs with a highway patrol officer.
Polished shoes for potential marriage feast.
Scrubbed candle holders with S O S.
Made thermos of tea instead of coffee.
Prayed to sunflowers for rain.
Read real estate terminology to Mozart.
Laughed at my face in someone else's mirror.
Listened to history evaporate inside a mirage.
Remembered skeletons and Buddhas
side by side, Thai monastery.
Picked mums, stole tulips from senior citizens' home.

Saw who was meant for me.
Recognized the curve of her spine underwater.
Heard bells, heard the striker empty its sound.
Dreamed that once beckoned I could not be refused.
Heard the blood of my love drumming, heard a gallop.
Saw the children running up.
Hummed poptune ecstasy in falsetto freeplay.
Walked through walls, lay down with laughter.
Lit the nave with bare bulbs of desire.
Practiced truthful genuflections and thankyous.
Dressed the altar with sheets and pillows.
Faxed home intricate floorplan of roofless house.
Received letter stating "Cancel Resistance, Listen!"
Looked to the stars for an end to my poem.
Flipped through pages of water inside my head.

Realized world leaders should hold dialogues
in nautiloid floating position
rather than sitting at tables.

Spoke long distance my inner reality.
Received a Yes.
Broke down on way to supermarket.
Returned with pancake batter instead of asparagus.
Watched snails migrate in sudden rain.
Called again to say hello.
Woke from trance dream of wrap around rivers.
Woke into her arms through high voltage life lines.
Began latest journal entry without using "I"
Drove record distance with tank on empty.
Recovered Mystery from the Great
& All Bountiful Vacuum.

Said Good Night, turned off the light
to illuminate sleep.
Said Good Day, remembered gratitude
Remembered praise   .   .   .

2:AUG:90 the ceiling's not sky nor
heaven nor the top of the head, not mind
nor the mouth's roof.. But the limit
of your THEORY, the limit of your BREATH
stretching in & out...the limit of your
ability to take a stand, Act, GIVE wo!

14: AUG: (everything stopped in sideways rain:
hurricane; trees; water thru windows:
~Electricity's off, wisteria Blown Down:
mind alive! Power ON!)

eye

write: Wee Don't Be so busy BEING.
Listen to the Boundaries Snore.
While the Eye tickles what's
                    Between.
Peel Back the Metaphor; Uncloak
    the Humming Bird from its
MIND FLOWERS... We're
Naked in infinity's ThunderHead!
Breathe deep the STaR that VANISHES
 Before the arrival
            of IT'S HEaT

About to Title a Painting for a Friend, I Write a Poem Instead

At ease, friend.
At ease with your shell.
Go ahead, touch the barking leaf.
Smell the black firs laughing.
Tie your shoelace
without looking up.

At ease
on the quick glacier we walk.
The crumbling slope, the Grizzly
half human.

It is a privilege
to build this fire high, unroll
the tatami and find
dry wood.

At ease
with everything
brilliantly dark.
There is no big word
to slow the poem.

Even the canoe suddenly whirling
in night's pond
smiles
in the moon's reflection.

Field Guide to the Body's Anatomy

Body's banquet is liquid sunlight
Spine is fossil cypress in the swamp of time
Head perches like a bird upon the soul
Eyelids close over antechambers of Triassic glow
Tastebuds dine on inner ear
Cheekbones reverberate with whatever we speak
Nose inhales alphabet pollen
Breasts are supernovae visible at high noon
Buttocks are two sides of one-same moon
Veins branch from arteries like Bombay streets
Shoulders once had wings
Body blinks an all-seeing bellybutton
Intestines run with gossip
Lungs play accordion song of visionary breathing
Crotch hides secret passageways in tangle of leaves
Rain falls from underarms
Ears hear the shape of aurora borealis
Feet are fins exploring prenatal depths
Limbs spiral out as Milky Ways
Pubic hair is all that's left of ancestral self
Mouth is a page turning in the breeze
Tongue rolls backward into heart's secret notebook
Stomach digests rhetoric and farts loudly
Legs fall as they walk, gravity rules
Brain writes earth movies, mind plays reruns
Belly and thighs can taste, bottoms of feet can smell
Blood turns the face red, bones may break
Flesh can be poked, pierced, cooked, penetrated
asked for, given, received, tampered with, made sacred
kept clean, stripped, dressed, masked, moved
kidnapped, stored, held in ransom, given a price.
Body fits precisely into body
Body wiggles from Eve's apple, grows old inside
the shadow of a child, becomes ghost and howls
Body sweats, glows in the dark, jumps, swims
shrivels, undergoes molecular change, barks, kisses invisibly
gives birth, continues in recombining forms.
Body is a porch to the soul's cabin
Body begins inside body, kneels in churches, stands
in synagogues, whirls in deserts, sings in graves

dances on pyres, floats down rivers
and rejoins the one-same sea
of the body's greater Body

Song of the Talus

— for Jim and Lenora

Permit me
to eye the escaping cloud, grasp at phantoms;
slide as far down as the scree takes me.

I'll carry a stone in my mouth
until silence is mine, climb and climb
until my arms no longer reach but hold
the star's center.

Permit me
terror of the world below.
To stand in the black zenith of the pinnacle
with the sun beneath my feet.
To forget what I know, and face the abyss
ever praising, with dignity.

Mt. Hesperus, Colorado
Late Summer 1989

14 OCT '89 ie: 2532

"walking is our Home, the Journey OUR MATRIMONY" (says my eternal child playmate; my all-sea-ing magic DOUBLE)

SHE: whose smooth branches are Paradise where the Butterfly hides... SHE: whose Right (rite) forms the LEFT of Me...

SHE: whose Lips speak the Question to My Answer... whose taste gives BACK. My OWN...

it's the Song of this tree that begins Me... it's the Heat of the Leaves that fires the BREEZE

ALMA

Prologue in the Key of C

I want to write
unsayable towers of cloud, wind tunnels
inside the hand, days and months without name,
fish luminescing in curtains
opening into windows always asking
us further as we touch.

I want to write
the desert's unfound stones
darkened by eclipse, the moonstruck eye
ascending through blue-quick lightning.

I want to write
you and me lost in the body's secret extensions,
here just one brief instant
to be completed in the salt and oxygen
of a single flash — as Scorpius swims from
the Milky Way, as mystery beckons from the mirror
whose depth ignites my pen.

I want to write
whirling twilight inside a conch,
how your breathing enlarges my being
how your name liquefies space,
incessantly revealing its awakened shape.

I want to write
the how of you, the where of you
the sweet amber of your wakened face,
the glazed cry inside me as meteors stand still
in the dampness of our single eye.

I want you to know
openly and vividly this poem
I do not know, this door inside the door,
this fragrance pounded from a dream,
how the moon suddenly darkens
and in the darkness we speak the unspoken
and in the unspoken begin to meet.

Total eclipse of the full moon,
Autumn Equinox, 1989

To the Angel Half Fire Half Snow

Please
wear your pearls indoors today. Sit with your legs back
and skirt pulled up over your head.

Let
the whole feather show, the bliss of your throne
catch fire as you elevate in recombining forms.

Let
the perfect zero of each breast, the blue forest
of spinning tongues give back the grace

I was born with
before the pious tied my hands
with their simulated fervor.

Please
uncloak your seventy thousand veils
of ambergris and hyacinth.

Guide me with repeated supplication
that I may drink your snowy darkness, taste
your fire — and never thirst again.

Kathmandu, 1989

Two Bodies

Our edges meet beyond us.
I can't say who I am, only give shape
to the rock and air from which I've been.

Our dance multiplies in flight.
We undress inside a tree of lightning, wake
from a thunderclap, exit into fire.

Our bodies don't understand names,
only know the fountain of blood
that echoes their beginning.

I see you in the silence we begin from.
You find me, too
On the balcony of an identical room.

For This We Come

Obedient to the luminous ray
that evaporates the time-stopped edge,
we begin our stroke.

Inside the hypnotized eye
we empty the boulevard and multiply
into a kingdom of waving trees.

I am your offspring, you the ultimate sea.
A mantra of silent pirouettes
that informs the dream.

In a heatwave, love burns without shadow.
Along a moonstruck outline
we swell and become thin.

Under the tea kettle are flames,
every essence hides in steam. The world
isn't exactly seen.

For this we come:
to breathe and stop still, to find form
behind our names.

Song for Autumn

Warm me as the weather chills,
drink deep this antlered heat.
Carry me through the world's gate
that I may taste a deeper sea

Lift me, crest to crest
inside your flame
Confound me
that my journey be invigorated

Confront me
that questions always be there
Calm my breath
within the swirl

That I may hear every dimension
of the water's sound
Through you
let me love all that's given

Let us ripen in solitude
to face the multitude
Let our bodies fuse
and weigh less than their single shadow

In firm, wet soil
may every undertaking be realized
Let our love find rest
in a clear, deep shore

And our house be buoyant
in unforeseeable waves
Let our imaginations merge
    and our hands give meaning to this song.

21 March 1989

Hear! Twoday! Thee Sol breaks from shadows like an egg to reseed Earth ship as it sails along faster than the sound of speed, quicker than a year of light. & Rejoice~! You are a hand through your own mirror; outside is the inside of another outside; set thee table with bowls of see food.: & Don't say "Here is our work" when We are the work to be done.

Cancel Resistance! Listen! Become the ache in the Volcano's gut, to sea's lost wave quieting away to sea:

XI.

NEW POEMS
(1991-94)

"I hear my footsteps coming back
Along the track where no one has been."
— Apollinaire

Dos Sueños entre
   de mi vida entre
SOL, NUBE, Y ABUNDANCIA
      de LA HONDA OBSCURIDAD:

#1: I cLimBed a Long flight
   of stairs to small N.Y.C. loft,
bare of Everything save for BED, Lamp
   & chair... & there He was
      PRACTICING: JOHN COLTRANE
            Hymn-
            SELF.

AFTER awhile, in
muted AMBER LIGHT
diffused by oilcloth
      WINDOW
         Shade
   he turned &
   asked: "AND YOU?"

WHEN I Read
Him My Poem, he Eyed
Me gentle BUT intense
& SAID: "Ah, You
   Like to start up
         High too."

#2: YEARS
      LATER
   I TOLD this to MiLes
      & he said ABSOLUTELY NOThing.
      He had his Back toward me
   & WHEN He finally turneD Around
   I could See he was a PRIEST.
He had me Kneel
   & gave me HoLy Communion
FROM his HORN.

Sending Out the Ghosts

Ghosts leave traces everywhere.
Orange peels in the drain, a sudden spot
of wine on the table. An old clunky tune
played after midnight on the piano.

Evict them by letting them know
you've lined several stones in a row and if by morning
one is moved, they'll have to go.

No more faces in the fire, nor draft of passing feet.
No more strange whiskers in the sink
nor fingerprints on the cup.

Rub your hands counterclockwise
chanting o u t 's to the sound of rain.
Burn sage under the bed.

It's polite to let each ghost know
you've drawn the line.

That your lover's not for hugging. Your manuscript
doesn't need any finishing touch. That each dish
is okay exactly where you've placed it.

Shake pollen from sunflowers.
Mix it with spittle. Make a paste and lather
every doorknob.

Quietly help the woodvine up its trellace.
Examine the skylight, the shutters, each window.
Without ghosts, the moon shines through.

Natural History of a Whitened Landscape

We met before angels had wings
or heaven a name, or the eye an eyelid
with which to close during a furious kiss.

We stole from the center of a star
before horses had tails, or fish thought of swimming
or the moon could possibly eclipse.

Most precisely,
we were a marvelous echo in the chamber of birth,
a foamy liquid between shore and ship.

A singular translucent note
making its way
before such a thing as night or day.

Our bodies
weren't heavy with shoes.
Our lives hadn't been hinged to metaphor.

We were a fluttering edge
lit from behind by a luminous design
not wanting to be named.

An empty reverberation
uneasily considered by scientists today
   — and hardly mentioned by theologians:

An ephemeral constant
lost to memory . . .

Yes, a wild riparian glance.
A vibrating eye, alert and serene.
A starry lip at the mouth of chance.

You were to me and I was to you
a sweet untranslatable wave, two facing paths
in the secret joy of our mutual heat.

From Desert Journals / 1991

Open eyes, close them—same scenery is there.
Desert is mirror, physical replica of the self undressed.
In rippled heatwaves, in dancing vortex of thermal updraft,
mind stops, unnecessary baggage evaporates.

With lightness the eye takes hold.
Rainshafts play tricks with cinder cones. Antlers click.
Thunder echoes. Volcanoes rise, unpredictably disappear.
Lightning makes upside down song notes of neck hairs.

Life as psychic merge, waking & dreaming
where heart mind rock mirage all overlap, landscape made portable
as its spirit enters the body, becomes humanized
finds dwelling—sings out through the flesh.

Geography begins from within, erupts from imagination
becomes real as we walk, fades as we turn, continues
to be remembered as strange telegraphic teletype spelling out
metaphors for a world beyond ours.

Coyotes yip. Stars ripple in waterpockets.
Lizard tails leave wandering petroglyphs inside bootprints.
Mind zigzags with magnetic seismography mapping heart's trail.
Vocal chords vibrate liquid mandalas into Cassiopeia's throne.

Geography beckons our imagination with symbols
for another reality. We, the imperfect reverse of a place made real
in visions. Topography? An esoteric Braille read by foot, eyed by toes
savored by cellular galaxies up and down the vertebrae.

I breathe deeply this sweet desert night
inhale anonymous constellations   exhale blinking embers
from the Dream Maze. May they seed the universe
make dandelions yellow, meat red.

The poem?   Topographic   typographic.
Bear path, dolphin wake, endless switchbacks over wind-ripped
top-of-the-planet peaks. Crowcall, freefall. Sea foam off tsunami.
Unending advance of sand dune in the brain.

—*Delicate Arch, Utah*

E Train to Spring from Port Authority
Down Beneath Manhattan's Floating Electric Island Maze

Look look look at this
voltage-wired undersea maze of tile-dripping
arteries, the port-wine darkness, green folds of sludge
from all colors, every sex, shape and race
planted there above   — O labyrinth
of screeching wheels   cyclopean headlights,
echoing stench into which one descends
and for a moment is married to another
who is numberless in the multitude
where one rides the glistening tracks, fused
with shadows   endlessly multiplied.

Look at this guy now
under Port Authority, down the sleeper-bundled steps
on the poorly-lit fluorescent platform
in black beret and rain-soiled overcoat, playing *Carmen*
on a violin under his whisker-stubbled chin, the *Toreador March*
delicately drifting like spun glass
through the hissing pick-axed capillaries,   90 cents
of spare change in his open case, bushy eyebrows lifting
up and down, pupils unrolled deep into their lids
and a bum opposite him jig-dancing cross-leggedly
in torn canvas shoes and woolly cap,
              precariously close to the tracks.

Confusion, of course
sublime wonder and cave-deep terror
joy and stumbled glory
in the beamed cordage and riveted, shadowed ribs
beneath Manhattan's floating electric island
up there brightly moored.

Look, a Bombay man
in fiery turban, smoke issuing from coat cuffs;
   a priest in green tennies;   a broke-down knit-cap
Arabian cab driver with harlequin   in checkered leather
and platinum hair,   whose umbrella handle curves
into the head of a smiling goose.

And then, the "E" train . . . Penn Station
14th   Washington Square   — hurried rapport
quick chiseled fragments of people's lives
— success, infidelities   questionable worth
        of metals   stocks   bonds
flashy costumes   pent-up scent of jasmine
green flesh under copper amulets,
purple-lipped lady   speeding toward prohibited
Mecca; child-woman with soft magnolia face speaking
Amsterdam accent;   a white-gloved stand-up comedian
who isn't very funny   and a cane-tapping blindman
making way through swordfish and celery,   someone's fist
clenching a see-through shower cap
filled with tokens   Tiger Balm   mozzarella balls
mentholated sweets   and fire opals.

Perhaps it's the heated silence,
the multi-lipped ever-changing passenger shadows
in squares of fluorescence   the blood light
of dark blue,   bodies — all teeth and branches
distorted, whirling   — or the sudden inward-quiet symphony
of what everyone's thinking;   the dotted menagerie
quickly tumbled and emptied . . . but I think I see
Joan of Arc   Coleman Hawkins   a longlost
Seneca orator   the son of Atahaulpa   Gertrude Stein
playing the accordion,
                a kid from Spanish Harlem
half weeping exploding icicles of human speech
along the occult underground rails
surrounded by salty-sweet change-of-body scents
    leotard youth   sequined cleavage
of filmclip conversations,   until . .

Suddenly, Spring Street   — a quick stop,
infinite zero of bald heads flashing in diagonal squeeeeze
of pushing hips, slanting whinny
as Coltrane soprano-whine of wheels and brakes   SLAM
and players   actors   polarized currents
of migrating pedestrians distortingly interweave
and magically, in claptrap rhythm
of exiting upward-flowing riverheels, rotate
through constellations of metal doors

and find their way   OUT
        up stairs   into dusk-heralding
            mother-of-pearl light.

Then, in private silence,
in flesh-cage wrappings under bobbing umbrellas,
this marriage of everyone   parting
this dark-tunneled gypsy-pilgrimage not seated, but
walking through a net of iridescent bubbles
anonymously blown from a stuffed bear   into the air
between 6th & Broadway,   over
rainwet newspaper-flapping sidewalks
        — bubbles everywhere   and a Chinese girl
bending to swoop them,   gather them
                into a little wire basket.

And look, the falsies
all in a row skyward pointed,   toothpaste   hairpins
        matchbook devils between fake turquoise
Taoist mountains   —all for sale in the open-air market:
Viking ships in old vinegar bottles
        bent-knee made-in-Taiwan plastic Charles Atlases
glass Christmas ornaments   paperweight Elvis
Presleys,   a chocolate Brooklyn Bridge
        and sad, orphaned look-alike
                Statues of Liberty.

And in Little Italy,
or along Canal Street   it picks up again:
the wave-swell of poor hulks;   the bookbag-toting schoolkids;
piano mover   vegetable ladies   a man wheeling
manta rays across Mulberry;
humanity   —all of us, fat and small
the guy on stilts   chestnut seller
        falafel vendor   goldfoil calligrapher
        coughing faucetfulls of little dethroned princes;
all of us fashioned from whatever creed or sex,
        myriad shapes   every size and color
set down from above, rubbed from genie lamps,
lifted from the pink froth of the chain-ringing sea:

Neptunian   Brazilian   Afro-Asian . .
      . . you from Mozambique, you Mercedes
you Jacques,   you from Huehuetenango
                    you Prettyhorse, you Mohinder
you from Philly,   you from Fez
        . . you Vladimir, you Nicanor
you from Kingston, Belfast
      Komandorskie, Shongopavi . .

Window washers   fork lifters
Born agains   war protesters   atheists
between dandy ladies speaking in perfumed tongues:
you cinnamon face   you milkweed   you tarantula general
you frog eyes   peering from dirty-brick building
you Venus,   neo classical relief in ordinary clothes,
shoulders tattooed with arrows and clouds.
You   the champagne drinker eyeballing me from
fifty-five stories above,   you beneath step-down streets
port-guzzling from twisted paper bag,
      you like a reed   a windchime, a dis-
                              located wave.
Island, O island electric,
shored with flashing ships and lopsided fireboats
      tonnage of silk and coal   wheat and weapons
            blue dots of bridges   . steely harpstrings
lifting callgirls and rabbis whalers hermaphrodites
            lip-smeared lovers   — Eskimo Otavalo
      Soweto   businesswoman   arms smuggler
librarian   flame eater   hipswinging transvestite Moses
monk   magician   partially-veiled Muse
      speaking through the rearview mirror   — Osiris
      in the lap of a cigar smoker;   the backseat
handcuffed dream   confused rays
      of fractured magenta   split lips   black eyes
            kicked groins   face of Mingus   voice
        of Billie Holiday   scissor-stenciled
sharp-angled shoulders and pelvises,   paper-cut
mosaic of silhouetted heads, cloudy rush
of neoprene feathers, propaganda heroes
      peeling from doorjambs and broken statues . . .
            barn shingler   shipping clerk
        tollbooth lady   child blowing kisses

with Botticelli eyes   — clockdials   fire switches
angry chains, whispered names, gullied
    concrete city canyons,   Yes!

Whatever hurries whatever refuses
whatever falls   whatever fails   whatever loses
itself in awe   in flame   in consum-
mate action   — it is one and same,
all exchange identical secrets, share damp stone
share penthouse, share burial grounds
hunger   darkness
inside the fingers, fleshy properties
surrounding the soul.   Anonymously
we marry   —and are beautifully
                                        One.
It *is* as Whitman said:
    "Outlines . . do you see o my brothers and sisters?
It is not chaos or death   — it is form, union, plan.
          It is eternal life.   It is Happiness."

. . . the riveted past, the fluid
present   the dusk-anchored, dawn spreading
    future,   Yes I am
        heaven-high   under-
ground,   subway trekking, from Port Authority
to Spring,   past Penn Station and 14th
    past Washington Square,   on the "E" train
        exiting ever so absolutely crazed
    into Manhattan's floating
            rhythming
                electric maze.

the MIRROR Broke the CLOUDS RoLLeD the LaVa cRacKeD the Steam BLew

the wiLLows CHoKeD the wateR FeLL

In chaos useD we KisseD & MaDe a Nest in the Moon's BReast:

it was gentLe peRsuasion, it was CoNey IsLanD.

2 horses SwaM stReaM FRoM the Main & Ran: in LoVe's pulse JoineD, they RoDe the RiDe of ContRaRies & DeLiGHt weeping in Joy, SeeDeD by soRRow they BeCame a in GoD's

Listen, the Promise is Hidden

Look at the yellow rose
on the desk, its long stem breathes
even after it is cut, the scissors on the floor
keep trimming the leaves
of the book
even after you've stepped out the door.

The rose drops a petal
and another
as I write. It has a mouth and an eye
that sings a plaintive
solemn song, a beam that holds true
between the jagged precipices
          of our work.

We know
out of necessity form flares;
concentration loosens
        a tiny crystal knot, showers
the alchemic bubble with a sun-drenched tune;
bursts the web whose silk-thin
        seedhairs mingle the metaphor
with astonished drops of dew.

Look. The round
floating microcosms of petals
testify to something larger
than the mystery our brushstrokes
reveal.   The promise is hidden
like the faraway center
of the rose   under chambered folds
                of yellow.

Listen.
There is a song, a half-open parable
leads us deeper and deeper
  through the inkwashed vertigo
        that surrounds.

Of Energy, Ebony, Rosewater & Lime

What do I know
Pondering Han Shan's oblivion dream
Or the afterglow of Lao Tzu's comet
Extinguished in a pond
Except that tonight the breeze is clear
And in it the 400-quadruple-billion
Possibilities in the Holy Mother's eye
Are void of roads and headlines.

It is an enigma
How every time you wear your coat indoors
It begins to rain,
How the clock discards its tick
        And the banging gate takes up its pace.
It is by no coincidence
That as we speak a spider threads a walkway
Into apocolyptic folds as you iron your clothes
Or that by themselves
        The trees lift and begin to spin.

And I'd say "karma"
But we'd have a cliché, or I'd say "uncertain"
        But we'd have the debris.
Clearly, the banging gate is only in our heads;
For the cat in her basket of cloves, though open-eyed
Refuses to awake.

It's not captivity, but the freedom to leave
That's brought you here,
Not the pencil on the desk rewriting
    The fragile majesty
        Of the erect eye
But you,
Spreading love's hieroglyph
        On the hypnotized sheets.

You wore all black
The night we began our feast.
You were falling between rhododendrons,
        A pulsing snowflake

As Orion's belt loosened
After we crossed the exposed bedrock
        On the way home
from the tanka painter's hut.

You drew bathwater
Into a galvanized tub   flavored it
With deodar   and sat in the steam
Like a naked hinge.
    A sack of pears in the corner
Echoed the pure adrenaline of your sweat.

Afterwards   (crumbling cork
                        floating in white wine)
A flame X-rayed your shape
Inside a luxurious hexagram of pomegranates
On your open kimono.
You were the child obsessed with notebooks,
Green fountain pens, the presence
Of woodsmoke and amaranth.

This morning,
An absence of implication
        And nothing to surmise or define.
An egret lifts and begins its glide
In dawn's afterglow.

On the balcony you pour jasmine from
The Karmapa's teapot,
Chant the verandah into snowfields,
Each sound a demolished transparency
That multiplies your face into deep lines
        Of railways and rattling window frames.
Metaphors of rapid speed that fog the lyrics
        As I beg the glass to quit reflecting;
But it continues to forge another,
And another of you.

And I say Ebony, I say Tara
Sprinkle rosewater over the secret parts of Kali
Eat the lime from the somnolent tree
On the dry hillside of childhood's play.

You are here now, you've come back.
In the smoke of brushfires
Your cassock unveils the lost order
That opened the aperture of our dream.
It's not done
    It's never completed
It's not going to rain.
            This moment's not absences
But consequences   unbreathable pools
Heady wine of rioting syllables,
      The ache of your breasts
           In the castle of each hand.

No, not done
      But here, just beginning
Right here, in the door . . .
           That familiar head of hair
              That fragile liberty —

From Himal Journal

— Annapurna Circuit, Nepal

Adventure does not drive me.
Nor reason. Something in the genes
alchemically combines with impulse
& sets forward the feet — into thin flint-scented air,
    oxygenless realm of creaking stone
        large-knuckled pillars of ice.

Heights constantly change,
loss of gravity challenges my grip.
This flesh I wear is of the slow-paced race,
awkward in vertical trudge over ancient reefs
& fossil shores once skimmed
    by ancestral fin
        in horizontal glide.

Ultimately I accept the thin air,
feed on stellar equations, thrive on endless designs
of bronze & violet inside my eye.
Body is a walking sutra, skull throbs
    with storm, ancestral memory
        — seeds of the unborn.

Lao Tzu's poems are agates in a tarn.
Bodhi Dharma's meditation wall, a glacial face
mottled with debris   — my erratic breathing
    primal wheeze & heave
        of dissonant vocabulary: something
of the mother tongue: rudder of song, heatwave
in a field of ice — a chant far from mind
        deep in the Blood Garden of the body.

Spectator, participant,
I am the face of everything seen:

Behind a weathered pole-frame ladder
a stately woman in Tibetan dress combs out
wet strands of shimmering hair to dry.
Around a corner, a sudden lump of soiled rags

warms itself in crisp high-altitude sun:
an old man　— forlorn, mouth caked with spittle,
eyes shut with mucous.　He can't see but knows I'm here.
Knows my race, my transcience　—& waves me away.
Above him looms the mountain's crystal presence:
　　　　Anna — sustenance.
　　　　　　Purna — goddess.

Stranger here, stranger
back home —I walk to rid of accumulation,
regain perspective, become small in the shadow
of a massif larger & more mysterious
than anything dreamed.　If there be duty connected
with this journey, it is to give significance to it.
To ascend each switchback, not by foot
　　　　　but by power of a humble song.

Cold, soaked with sweat,
I absorb the sunrise:　violet-green atmosphere
　short breaths　5-7-5　ledge-to-ledge leaps
improvisational circumam-
bulation around a whitewashed cairn
whose fluttering prayer flags
　　　　　transform wind into mantra.

Nomad. Harvester.
The body traverses solidified fire,
sunlight webbed in chlorophyll veins,
lichen colonies　untamed in vertical folds.
Home is exactly where I stand,
alphabets planted wherever tracked
　　— grain & chaff carried in cuff;
　　　　　glued to the sweat of the sole.

The pass is in the heart.
We shall always be crossing it, acclimatizing,
gauging the slope.　At the summit
time halts, becomes a concentric ripple
inside the eye.　When it opens, it opens
with the very first moment of the world.

In it, I'm simply here,
a concentrated semblance
set to flame.   Truth is beauty,
     the elemental reality that surrounds.
Doubt is that ragged gap flushed with sunlight
through which I've hiked.

From peak to peak, snow banners
feed infinity fine sparkles of jeweled dust.
It is here I begin.
Humble, pedestrian,   at crest
          — becoming light with the climb.

Guess, Feel, Doubt, Brighten the Air
With Your Nocturnal Self

It is a long way through the sand
to the mouth of the canyon.
Trails wander like veins inside the skin.
Night overturns its malachite bowl on the world,
    — each star inscribed with a doorway.

From where, these blue rafters of light?
What animal in the torso
        begs the ark from the sky?

Each of us spins like plankton
in the head of a comet,   wanting to make,
 wanting to love,
      we hear only the beating in our chests
& flounder in the heat,   remembering a flood
     or inventing water that will never come.

Every day
we share the same air
breathed by two lovers in bliss
or blackened by the executioner's call.

A few wake from insomnia,
bodies hemorrhaging at the canyon's mouth.
A few realize their wings
    — go dizzy with lifting, cry like babies
in the flaming channel of birth,
& suffer no more the voice
that caged the heart.

Follow them out!

Turn your hands over and over
until the palm lines don't exist.
In a transient moment not of your choice,
take flight   — have nothing to say
& in the finding
    have no need to find yourself.

No enemy is here,
no boundary smuggles its wall into sleep,
no battle goes on fighting.
You are beyond the hard matter
          you believed real.
You have seen, & found
          your breath sweet.

You have exited
the worrisome screen.
You can guess, feel, be open, always
beginning. Let the heart swell
          without need to measure
               or understand.

With time to go nowhere
          you are everywhere, weaving
resilient fibers into a strong design
of light balancing dark;
               you have courage to let come
what you want to go, making use

Of the labyrinth's confusing trails,
finding edge after edge to complete the middle.
          You are home, you are fluid, you are
chaste in the death of emergence, energizing
the world with your gaze.

Every direction
holds a space of blue to recognize
and submit to. There's a half smile on the lips
in the mirror   —fragrance drawing
                         vision from sleep.

That woman inside the woman
stands up in you now, & the one lastly
revealed reveals the god in you, all the strange gods
that gave you warning   —& then clearing
to step forth from the mire
          in which the uncourageous placed you.

I Forgot Myself Last Night

I'm still there
in that city of knife throwers and glass heels
biting your grenadine ear in the blue wind of diamond row
I haven't left the velocity of our Yes
the dust of your settling rose

That was me
in the undertow of midnight sun
between vibrating canyons of polished steel
I was there taking a long swig of the conspirator's drink

In the hematite of your bones
in the stone birds of Magritte
in the trembling discotheque
    in the batik of spinning tongues

I left myself
        —completely there

Under cold-fingered icons
in ricocheting fables of argon
in Blake speaking from stairwells
in Bach synthesized in the silence
    after the howl of the Lexington Ave Express

I was that one—

Who wasn't in this body
Who stepped into the footprint of hunger,
the Harlem of your eclipse. Who sat in the late night diner
of imagination's rebellion, smelled the gasoline
a thousand feet below; drank the oxygen
of your adrenaline flame

That was me, not this one
but the one still there in the whitewater of your stream
in the the open scent of your subterranean rhyme
at the edge of the phantom gate, in the prolonged stroke
of lightning that flashes backward
to your incarnate amnesty

In all of this
and everything that appears
I disappear

In the ash of tourmaline
I spiral upward, in the triple shot of tequila
you down me. Along the double line of Fifth Ave
I scatter my false I.D.
In the confessions of the innocent
I walk forward

On the pillowcase
is an eyelash, in the soundbox of your breast
language irresistibly ignites
Our lives live
each truth revealed in sleep

Yes, I forgot myself
I'm not here, I was never in this body
I left myself there
I disappeared in the window of your minaret
in the eager drawback of your pendulum

I became
     a wild seed
     in a thirsty ravine.

No Superlatives Please

Just the gone feeling
of being exactly one with crows and hummingbirds
in the half harvested field of water breaking
from your rosy silence.
There's not really a lot to it
except to do what you say. If you're a poet
sire delight through what you write.
If you're a vagabond fry the fish with its eye
pointed up. And if you are in Changmai drink
heavy of unidentified tea.

I've placed two hydrangea flowers
in your hair over breakfast, and helped tie a filagree amulet box
at the smooth blue throat under your face.
The Borneo bead sellers are on the sidewalk two doors down.
The women pleating palm leaf votives are open legged
between jackfruit and custard apples in their kiosk.
And on a sawed-off tree trunk
the woodcutter dozes.

Shall we go back to that place
where the fat buddha boy with protruding ballbearing
navel painted with milk-white swastikas
holds out, in eternal yoga position, a little wooden sign
saying "Antique Sunset from Hot Shower Room"
or tease the rice field scarecrows at the intersection
with the rambutan tree shedding leaves on a stone Garuda
ideographed with lichens picturing strange recollections
written by Valmiki inside his 14-year anthill retreat
or read about the latest evildoings
of the Indonesian police state
in the Alligator Cafe?

At dusk — quite faithful to its usual
mother-of-pearl, the lantern man proceeds into the rising
lopsided moon, bamboo stick dangling with froglegs.
And with every twist and creak of the neighbors' lovemaking
and the plipityplop of the old lady on the can
we laugh unwantingly as if inside an hourglass
where all is falling sound

of feathers from pillows plucked by mice
during sleep. Or something quite soundtrack-like
such as that Taiwanese woman
inflight from Surabaya to Yogjakarta through monsoon
stormheads bumping precariously
from 25 to 15 to 10 to 5 thousand feet
screaming out terror, so much sounding like blissful orgasm
and dark ecstasy — that the whole fuselage
feared and climaxed right along with her
until the pilot brought us to the tarmac safely
and all turned hot and green, orchid centers singing,
black jellies of open sewers moving, at that hour, goldenly
right along, and every tin roof a chime of burnt orange, dripping
ghostlike rain pendants, our room peeling
robin's-egg blue, stained amber
from decades of smoldering votives.

Today
I won't go for my mail.
No news from the outside, nor kretek puffs
of nipple-dark smoke. You've got my shoes, I've got your socks
and here we are both barefoot in Wang Wei's Moonflower Shop,
these names and incidents all true. The floating rings
and chunks of color in the maltmaker's *es campur*
might have been hallucinogenic stones
or deer antler ground to a Turkish-fine Java
and the *becak* driver on the monsoon corner is a wiry archangel
inside his tent of rain-pebbled plastic, an apparition
in a transparent death shroud.
The bus to Borobudor is waiting. The plane to Ama Dablam
already off the ground. The Vietnamese woman we met
barebreasted on the wharf in Ko Pipi has appeared again,
her apocolyptic apsara voice auspiciously rearranging
bat shadows on the sidewalk.

"And I am glad for everything
beyond the normal and how we choose it" you write
as I look over your arm and feel the backside
of your yellow thigh swollen tight
with the sting of a tropical bite, a map of dusk,
a ceiling of forest, a fluorescing ring
of wine-sweet liquid from under your arm

on a summer dress. This is the local express,
this is the alchemist ant eating the crumbs
of tropical wood from which the flying mermaid
simultaneously combing her hair and brushing her teeth
is made. Call it kismet, or what was it you said
about the note Coltrane hit, Stokholm, '63?

I want to caress endlessly
every square centimeter of light rippling through
the air today, and not need to call it something
or look for it over there, or eat from it in my lap
but foresake the superlative
and be faithful to the enhancement
of an already-formed perfection, a shared fidelity
of mistaken identities within the engaged obsession
of the moment.   Coomeraswamy called it "Perpetual
uncalculated life in the present."   Alan Watts wanted to know
"Does the light in the refrigerator really go off
when you shut the door"   — and you, dear friend
remark that your identity is complete
in the fury and delicacy and dead petals of the smashed offerings
of the world, as is, and isn't with all that's to be said
already said once before, and we can all turn our shit
into gold, drink down deep flame of darkcave desire
to resurrect green sapling of innocent youth
by entirely living just one moment as pure
foreplay, making meat grinder of mind demons
using one glass daily of wine to raise good cholestral level,
through all these shadows, through all these years
through all these bones, a great need
to unpsychoanalyze those rare blossoms
stuck to our dirty heels, see shavings of iron oxide
in the greens of the eyes, no option but to remember
everything you want to learn
you already know.

— Ubud, Bali

234

I Reconstruct Her as I Touch
I Disappear as She Alights

Over the years she's appeared as Parvati, Guadalupe,
Our Lady of Sorrows, Saraswati and the Virgin of the Swan.
She's fallen asleep on my shoulder on the bus out of Riobamba.
And curled up on the concrete waiting for the Night Express
in Allahabad. She stood in the heat with a cold plate
of jasmine, making wreathes at Pashupatinath.
That was her at the rusty spigot with a plate of tangerines.
She had gold fillings, she had missing fingers.
She had a bouquet of thunderbolts between her knees.
She was carved from pure alabaster, breasts and womb
darkened by the touch of countless mendicants
in the back alleys of Rishikesh. She rode a tiger, stood
on a half moon, rose from a conch. Her crown was spiked
with narcissus. Her lacquered arms spread from royal blue
sewn with kernels of wheat. Her music was fragrant,
her pendulum warm, her face darkened
by centuries of afternoon sun. She swam in incense,
pondered the catacombs. At the River Krishna she held
an aluminum begging bowl between her eleven toes.
I saw her in Cuzco struggling under a sack of charcoal,
the child orphan in broken flipflops.
She was at the Met wearing glass heels, shouldering
a pet monkey, making eyes at Modigliani.
She was Padmi sorting cockles on the beach at Mahabalipuram.
That was her in moonlight on the Zócolo after the earthquake
holding a tiny pair of shoes. At Jemez she wore a necklace
of butterflies. She peddled tickets for the Monkey Chant
from her bicycle in Ubud. She hopped from a Vespa
in fluorescent veils late for a wedding in downtown Quito.
She was Kuan Yin at the modeling agency,
the beekeeper's daughter off the road in the weeds near Zion.
She sat up all night, the angel in white
at the children's psychiatric ward. She won 1st Place
at the Fancy Dance in Rough Rock. I saw her sift corn pollen
into the gold winter light of San Ildefonso. She had eyes for me
in Aleknagik, sat in the shadows after serving me
in Quetzaltenango, slept holding a flying fish on the curb
at Puerto Angel. I saw her, the Diva with black pearls,
Queen of Voodoo on Telegraph Avenue, the Apsara

in her spirit house beckoning monsoon clouds
from the South China Sea. She sold pomegranates
from an upside down umbrella in Mandalay.
Poured cement in Bombay for the New Taj Hotel
at less than 20 cents a day, poured warm milk
from a bucket in the fog of San Cristobal,
worked her way through the Monkey Forest
doing full body prostrations up the steps toward
Buddha's third eye. She placed a grain of rice on her spoon
and bowed to the ten-thousand gods of the Pure Land.
She topped frosties at the Creme Queen, she knelt on a broken
pew in old town, sat in a garden of fireflies and began a litany
to the Sacred Heart. She is everywhere, and here again tonight.
I see her lift a pen, shift in her seat, hammer a walkway,
scatter a path, send an embrace out of reach.
Her outline is a thirsty ravine. She shapes a burning letter
over my head. She is time slipped from shadow, chorus
inside a singer. Genesis heralding creator, finish line inside
the runner. Her mane shakes in the eye of the storm.
Her memory opens the phantom gate.
Her words wake the resin in a forgotten tree.
She is carnelian, she is fauve.
She is heliodor, she is jade. Her continent begs
with heated cairns. Her harbor hides the smuggler's ark.
Her violin plays a nuptial feast. She is the wife of no man,
servant of no self. She is a thousand questions
inside the answer, voice singing through Byzantine rain,
name disappearing in the gallop of a dream.
She is a luminous presence — that of someone who's seen
this world before. And come again
to give it greater meaning.

I reconstruct her as I touch, disappear as she alights.

An island of rhythm spreads over me.
She motions me to her doorway, folds the world
into a paper wing.

*Night Express
Krung Thep - Krabi,
Thailand*

ground is not Solid...
Questions full of AIR...
Earth Soft & moving
Shadows   WED   to endless
Design of
Stellar
Equations.

2 × 2 × 1

Spectator, participant; I am the face
of Everything Seen.
I am this "WE" inside this ☺ who is ME. I fly
my own cloud; seed my own Rain; One ♡, two
faces ~ WE form our own Son, hour
own moon Shine, & chant a Mother tongue,
rudder of SONG ♪♪ Heatwave in a field of ice
Deep in the BLOOD GARDEN of The BODY.

18 Aug
92.

Turning Fifty Poem

I am turning fifty,
lights out, moon full, no waves
   of dissatisfaction
        lengthening their pull.

I haven't written
any Baudelaire prosepoems
revered by scholars fattened on tenure
   — nor received retirement gift watch,
gold hands ticking
      glottal stops of unfetched dream.

I haven't been loyal
to any poetry company
      or boxed opera of partyline politics;
I knew I could grow jade in my bellybutton
be myself in breadlines
vulcanize tires, or entertain millionaires
in my time off
     from near-miss bullet wounds.

I'm glad to have escaped
Sister Mary Esther, who drew the human Soul
on 3rd-grade blackboard, then erased
chalked-in areas of grace
with strangely-cleaved, highly-suggestive
     pink eraser.

I confess,
that was me on the phone.
I hung up two times, just to hear your voice.
I spied on your behind
during stuffy afternoon floormat naps
   in Mrs. Hefflefinger's kindergarten class.

I grew up
stole mailboxes, sabotaged R.O.T.C.
joined Peace Corps,   & spiked
the Ecuadorian Bishop's monthly ration
of U.S.A.I.D. catsup

with cannibus.

I'll admit —
I engaged in substance abuse:
overpolished the nude siren on my Uncle's
green Dodge with Turtle Wax,
took long drags of hallucinogen smoke
face down in the Golden Triangle,
drank Ayahuaska in doused-fire darkness
        of Upper Amazon.

I am turning fifty
& had a paper route
        — just like Lawrence Ferlinghetti.
I put a firecracker in Mrs. DeLong's classifieds;
flipped through Playboy in eery darkness
of historic stone milkhouse,
got cozy with blonde telephone operator
            on Methodist basement pingpong table.

I have a degree
I have two degrees
        — graduated from college, worked
morning-shift Juneau cannery; invaded
book stores with fish scales & half-shut eyeballs
stuck to my rubber boots — watched people move,
        had sports & travel all to myself.

I won't brag.
Half a century's just a thin line.
There's two scallions, a carton of lowfat milk
& one package of quinoa tempeh
in the cold broken rays of my Sears refrigerator
        — tomorrow the mortgage is due;
            but I don't worry.

It's another great day
of life based on the Impossible.
I'll walk to the Holy Land,
buy a fat apple fritter & odorless soap, wash mis-
matched socks, float old ties down the sink.

I'll look in the mirror
& not get scared — say to myself
    This is me!   I cook my own meals,
play Parchisi, & love to wander
the impressive fur of my lover's
      high heels. I once heard
the Sitka Russian Orthodox priest's confession
in 40-below Volkswagon convertible
& stood nude in front of Eskimo girls before class
      after they stole my sweatlodge clothes.

It's absolutely true:
I'm fifty — & still can't roll a joint;
  haven't learned to draw hands or feet.
But I do a pretty good imitation
of people caught in traffic jams
talking on cellular phones, & sometimes stand
in front of automatic teller machines
      waiting for stamps.

No —
I am not Tantric apparition,
    one foot slaying ignorance
mouth spitting fire into void of ricebowl.
Nor born-again, Frisbee-throwing
      religious fanatic aiming
for the laps of young girls in bikinis.

I don't own pistol, subscribe
to newspaper; I'm not Saturday morning
religious nut coming undone at your door
  with Oogha Boogha shield & bloody
prankster crossbow, holding hand
of wind-up child with perfectly-combed hair
    toting hidden propaganda
in behind-the-back briefcase.

That is not me —

I am eternal sailor
riding boat prow, wave-splashed
above timberline, filled with brain storm

& multiple parody of crazed perspective.

I sometimes read poetry
for money — or money for poetry.
I've been caught using a thesauraus,
have spent hours trying to find
the Greek word for doom,
have even held jobs
      — delivered oxygen in Guadalajara,
tanned hides in Duluth, worked nightshift
art-ad paste up for Gloria Gorelick in Guayaquil;
taught graduate art classes
how to glue   — & 5th graders how to paint
the exact hue of arctic sun
          on a fresh catch of winter pike.

That's me
on page 9 of *Shadow Play*
greeting my daughter's friends in green cape
& pink jock strap.
I was the Cowboy from Phantom Banks.
    Those are my ivory teeth
on the floor, my dice in the teapot.
I haven't crushed a Black Widow since ten
in the morning.

I am a good Samaratin,
rescuing crickets from bathtubs;
examining huge purple seedhead
of sprouting Amaranth
          in backyard spinach patch.
I am the sad witness
of time spreading laughing roots
under bank vaults & mausoleums,
          Parthenons & emerald necklines.

I got married
    I got divorced.
Twenty years later I bring my lover
to meet the relatives — all retired from assorted
harpsichord factories, miscellaneous footwear
& Saginaw Steering Gear.

Here they come, struggling up from sagging chairs
to call her by my first wife's name
        — because dad hasn't had the heart
                to tell them

I am fifty years old
& sometimes rat my hair,
drive across the border
        — dance to Flaco, interrupt the opera
rattling chains in spittoons.

I know Shakespeare, so I'm okay.
I no longer battle with open verse, iambic pentameter,
suffer migrains over form & technique.
23,000 breaths per day is enigma enough for me.
There's no reason to throw cocktails
against white adobe walls
when the rug-peddler turned art dealer asks
    — *can you paint bigger? do you draw trees?*
            can you make them look old?

I am turning fifty
& haven't been famous,
        except when I broke the rearview mirror
off Liberace's pink Rolls
        in his Las Vegas museum.

My books have been shredded.
My horoscope's been read.
My hair looks like horns in the morning
but I'm not imprisoned by mistakes, homesickness,
mildewed futons — or bad breath
        in the starry depths of eros.

I've watched age ripen
into fewer words & longer laughter;
I love sudden thermals
        rising life above crumpled expectancies.
And though I look for profound truths
        & hold a sacramental view of Nature
I steal an occasional stapler, eat from shrines,

squeeze toothpaste from
       any point on the tube.

I got kicked out of Matisse
for pointing a well-sharpened #2 pencil
at three little goldfish in the Denver Art Museum.
I was the only one
      in a crowd of devotees to circumambulate
Kathmandu's famous temple, & come away
        with chewing gum on his shoe.

I'm fifty   — you can ask me.
I've watched a Komodo dragon eat
      someone's binoculars.
I've seen no man on the moon
but have seen thunder flash over fields of snow.
I've turned down wrong streets,
caught icy stares,
      climbed into empty Ferriswheels, spilled
things in dangerous places.

I had a temper tantrum
as late as 1972. I didn't take mushrooms
with Kumi, didn't marry
the starry-eyed Medusa, never mutilated
a cactus, just barely escaped the purgatorial realm,
      completed difficult math exams,
pulled tendons dodging fishy institutions
& farted in a revolving door
      just to take it out on the world.

Tonight
I sweep dust under carpets
of a floor I don't own. I've traveled the globe
& still get off on the same corner.
This is a true poem,
      only the names have been changed.

Tomorrow
I'll return to molecular dust
all part of me ten billion years before
I was born.   I'll pass the Statue of Liberty,

watch drug deals
      on Staten Island Ferry, climb
Empire State Building,
hear eternal updraft
      of slow-motion Broadway Boogie Woogie;
watch black sun ricochet
      from Vietnam Memorial
          into Abe Lincoln's face.

I'll rinse my flesh
      in sidewalk street fountain;
hear Washington Square reggae prophet
chant down Babylon; watch body dance
with wise old resilience
      to fragrant discord of rap beat,

And at last catch up to my kids
who've long outgrown puberty. That's my son
auto rotating from pearly thunderheads
in Sikorsky dream chopper
        all primitivo, full of hope
in feathered helmet
      & blue ampersand goggles.

That's my daughter
with henna smile & knees of smoke.
Green length of subtle
      gold falling to ballroom floor,
clear stars & frightened wind
      soothing the snow.

It all goes on.
Believe me. I am fifty years old
laughing at neighborhood dogs lift heads
& bark when I blow atoneal drone
      from my 2 a.m. Arabian conch.

I won't jump
another BMW bumper
   & set off parkinglot alarms
or sit face to face with barbershop televisions
     playing reincarnate Groucho.

I don't need to polish
my wingtips, win a Guggenheim
or take part in another ivory tower
      grease 'er up workshop.

I got sick of Victory at Sea
I know who poisoned Niagara Falls.
I saw God crying in a splintered barrel,
saw Buddha out-of-breath
fleeing men in white paper masks
pest-spraying orchards
      of ripening McIntosh.

I heard the little old lady
just like me, asking what to feed
    her Tree of Heaven.

After 18,250 days
of life on Earth, I don't mind snails
leaving iridescent trails
on the windows I just cleaned
or the gate banging on a moonless night;
but I can't handle normality.
      I'd rather not lose cranial juices
to writing routines, or walk
on New Age coals
          to prove my genes.

I understand some Indonesian
a little Japanese   — have loved in Spanish
& almost French, but I still make plenty of mis-
      takes in English, though
I have come of age, pay tax,
bury an occasional bowel movement
in waving heads of purple aster
    with tiny fluorescent shovel on camping trips.

I've walked the Bright Angel's abyss
into fossil-depths of the Great Unconformity,
plastered my feet with moleskin
in the Temple of Apollo, &
on a typical summer afternoon with my brother

installed a set of shocks
upside down — though didn't realize it
'til halfway across Nevada
        to the Golden Gate.

I am turning fifty,
        — fifty is turning me.
I still get high
on crooked eyebrows, dark mandalas
at the center of breasts   — but don't like
        trap-door minds 100 years younger than mine
obedient to monitors & backwards history books
who don't say who stole
        Shoshone desert for bomb tests.

I once ran for president
of my own Mutual Abberation Society;
watched corporate busybodies go blind
on the gangplank of reason;
saw Miles lift holy golden Eucharist
above desolate heads
        seeking ardor at Popejoy Hall.

Tonight,
    I am fifty years old
watching the wheel go round
        building my hearth from pyramids of light.
Out the window orange tanangers sleep
in weeping elms   — vultures digest
        roadside stink of meaty ignorance.

Cockroaches
clatter across kitchen sink;
but I'm not hungry for muscleman body,
painted toes, others' wives, monied life, what to do
        with receding hairline, absent tanline,
                wrinkled knuckles.

Instead,
I nurture Naples yellow
onto gessoed linen, sort tiny poems
from lover's hair — eat pink kernal

of samsara seed, sit erect under Green Tara moon
asking reflective light to soften
      bad-thought realms.

I'll rise early
   — weave honeysuckle trellis
through mind darkness
      of Superpower catastrophe
   — perform impossible yoga
with imperfect body   wrap leg
around leg in flexible, shifting
      Vertigo prayer:

"Our Mother
who art in Heaven
   — ring the glass chime
of subterranean possibility
    & pure state of mind de-
tachment"

Today,
fifty years old,
I am but a single rippled wingbeat
someone dreamed;
I see debris
    of old festivals — storm
  breaking
    into laughter
      at last.

Full lunar eclipse
November 1993

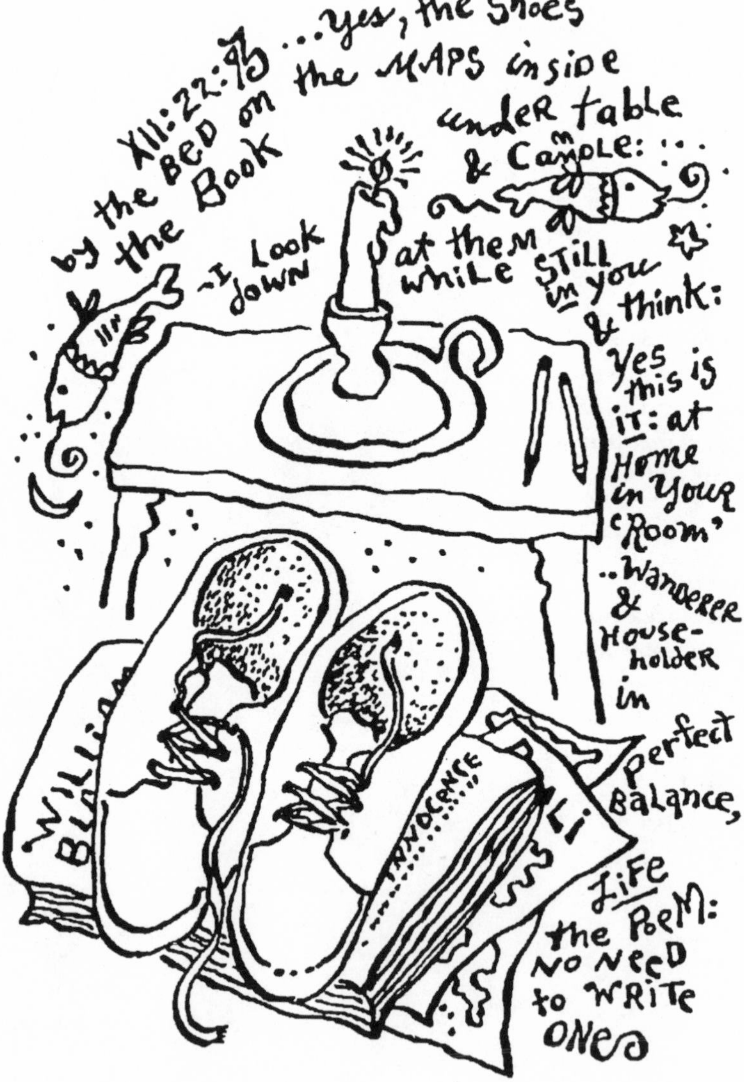

XII:22:93 ...yes, the Shoes
by the BED on the MAPS inside
the Book
under table
& candle: ...
~I look down
at them while STILL in you
& think:
Yes this is IT: at Home in Your 'Room'
..Wanderer & House-holder in perfect Balance,
LIFE the PoeM:
No Need to WRITE ONE
INNOCENCE

White Pine Press is a non-profit publishing house dedicated to enriching literary heritage; promoting cultural awareness, understanding, and respect; and, through literature, addressing social and human rights issues. This mission is accomplished by discovering, producing, and marketing to a diverse circle of readers exceptional works of poetry, fiction, non-fiction, and literature in translation from around the world. Through White Pine Press, authors' voices reach out across cultural, ethnic, and gender boundaries to educate and to entertain.

To insure that these voices are heard as widely as possible, White Pine Press arranges author reading tours and speaking engagements at various colleges, universities, organizations, and bookstores throughout the country. White Pine Press works with colleges and public schools to enrich curricula and promotes discussion in the media. Through these efforts, literature extends beyond the books to make a difference in a rapidly changing world.

As a non-profit organization, White Pine Press depends on support from individuals, foundations, and government agencies to bring you this literature that matters — work that might not be published by profit-driven publishing houses. Our grateful thanks to all the individuals who support this effort and to the following foundations and government agencies: Amter Foundation, Ford Foundation, Korean Culture and Arts Foundation, Lannan Foundation, Lila Wallace-Reader's Digest Fund, Margaret L. Wendt Foundation, Mellon Foundation, National Endowment for the Arts, New York State Council on the Arts, Trubar Foundation, Witter Bynner Foundation, and the Slovenian Ministry of Culture.

Please support White Pine Press' efforts to present voices that promote cultural awareness and increase understanding and respect among diverse populations of the world. Tax-deductible donations can be made to:

White Pine Press
10 Village Square • Fredonia, NY 14063

Other American Poetry from White Pine Press

Heartbeat Geography
John Brandi
ISBN 1-877727-40-7   256 pages $15.00 paper

Watch Fire
Christopher Merrill
ISBN 1-877727-43-1   192 pages $14.00 paper

Between Two Rivers
Maurice Kenny
ISBN 0-934834-73-7   168 pages $12.00 paper

Tekonwatonti: Molly Brant
Maurice Kenny
ISBN 1-877727-20-2   209 pages $12.00 paper

Drinking the Tin Cup Dry
William Kloefkorn
ISBN 0-934834-94-6   87 pages $8.00 paper

Going Out, Coming Back
William Kloefkorn
ISBN 1-877727-29-6   96 pages $11.00 paper

Jumping Out of Bed
Robert Bly
ISBN 0-934834-08-3   48 pages $7.00 paper

Poetry: Ecology of the Soul
Joel Oppenheimer
ISBN 0-934834-36-9   114 pages $7.50 paper

Why Not
Joel Oppenheimer
ISBN 0-934834-32-6   46 pages $7.00 paper

Two Citizens
James Wright
ISBN 0-934834-22-9   48 pages $8.00 paper

Poetry in Translation from White Pine Press

These Are Not Sweet Girls
An Anthology of Poetry by Latin American Women

A Gabriela Mistral Reader

Alfonsina Storni: Selected Poems

Circles of Madness: Mothers of the Plaza de Mayo
Marjorie Agosín

Sargasso
Marjorie Agosín

Maremoto/Seaquake
Pablo Neruda

The Stones of Chile
Pablo Neruda

Vertical Poetry: Recent Poems by Roberto Juarroz

Light and Shadows
Juan Ramon Jimenez

Elemental Poems
Tommy Olofsson

Four Swedish Poets: Strom, Espmark, Transtromer, Sjogren

Night Open
Rolf Jacobsen

Selected Poems of Olav Hauge

Tangled Hair
Love Poems of Yosano Akiko

A Drifting Boat
An Anthology of Chinese Zen Poetry

Between the Floating Mist
Poems of Ryokan